S0-DTA-794

Fine Flowers by Phone

The Essential Guide

FINE FLOWERS

to Ordering Flowers

BY PHONE

Long-distance

BARBERA BROOKS

THE ATLANTIC MONTHLY PRESS

NEW YORK

Copyright © 1989 by Barbera Brooks

All rights reserved. No part of this book may be reproduced in any form or by any electronic or mechanical means including information storage and retrieval systems without permission in writing from the publisher, except by a reviewer, who may quote brief passages in a review.

Published simultaneously in Canada
Printed in the United States of America

Library of Congress Cataloging-in-Publication Data
Brooks, Barbera.
Fine flowers by phone: the essential guide to ordering flowers
long-distance / Barbera Brooks.—1st ed.
ISBN 0-87113-266-4
1. Florists—United States.   2. Florists—United States—
Directories.   3. Cut flower industry—United States.   I. Title.
II. Title: Flowers by phone.   III. Title: Ordering flowers
long-distance.
SB443.3.B76 1989   88-8192   381′.4574592′025—dc19

Design by Laura Hough

The Atlantic Monthly Press
19 Union Square West
New York, NY 10003

FIRST PRINTING

To my daughter Charlotte

ACKNOWLEDGMENTS

I would like to thank my good friend Carl Navarre, who held my hand throughout the rigors of developing the idea for this book, and whose belief in both my idea and my ability to get the project done is something for which I shall always be grateful.

Steven Brooks was instrumental in helping me name this book, and I am grateful.

Larry Boucher, one of California's most successful high-tech entrepreneurs and a good friend, came to my rescue, saving me from the organizational nightmares inherent in a project like this by not only designing a computer system for my use but by teaching me how to use it.

Germaine Gioia and Bill Ribar developed a wonderful press kit and Eddie Celnick was more than generous in letting me use one of his spectacular photographs of an exquisite Pat Braun arrangement (Salou, New York) for use as a writing card.

Dick Turner, Director of Education at Strybing Arboretum, was immensely helpful with technical advice. Eric Cogswell and Bob Solley were instructive on aesthetic matters. Jean Thompson and Barbara Belloli of Fioridella are responsible for developing my appreciation for new ways of arranging flowers and teaching me that there is artistic integrity in lots of different styles, regardless of one's own personal taste. Tom Pritchard of Mädderlake gave timely encouragement all along the way, and gave specific recommendations on how to enhance the book's usefulness.

I also want to extend warm appreciation to Robbin Schiff for such a gorgeous cover.

But most of all, it's to Annie Hilliard, who tirelessly assisted me on the research, and to my editor, Marjorie Braman, who was always available to solve any problem I had, for her heartwarming dedication to the project, not to mention the hours she poured into vastly improving the script, that I owe countless thanks and appreciation. These two can be credited with assuring that this project got done.

Many thanks to my good friends in San Francisco, Betsy, Bonnie, Shawn, Debbie and Janet, who came to my rescue in domestic responsibilities whenever I was in a pinch, and to my family, for their continued interest and support. I especially appreciate my mother's enthusiastic willingness to share her endless list of contacts everywhere.

And lastly, to all the people I talked to all over the country who love flowers as much as I do and were willing to generously share their thoughts with me, I am deeply grateful.

INTRODUCTION

The need for a book like *Fine Flowers by Phone* first struck me when I tried to send flowers to a friend in the hospital in Cleveland without relying on a wire service. After three frustrating days of tedious phone calls, to find a good florist there, I realized I couldn't be the only person confronted with the problem of not knowing whom to call to insure high-quality arrangements with artistic integrity when sending flowers long-distance. My lifelong personal affection for the world of flowers had given me the desire to make a meaningful contribution to its well-being, and this project seemed the perfect way to do that.

Over the last fifteen years I've watched an aesthetic revolution transform the shape of flower arranging all over the country. We started to see flowers displayed individually in clear glass bud vases and scattered on dining tables or grouped on chests and coffee tables (Ronaldo Maia); or florabundant, country bouquets filled with wildflowers and meadow weeds that looked as though they had just been gathered from the garden and casually dropped into a vase in the front hall on the way to the kitchen (Mädderlake); or grand botanical tapestries of flowers and fruits reminiscent of Flemish paintings (Barry Ferguson). Whatever the style, the artless "round mound" look, still closely associated with the floral wire services, gave way to a new, more natural vitality. The measured heights and widths of Hogarth curves, triangles and pyramids, an approach that seems more suited to engineering than flower arranging, was replaced by an emotional and artistic vision, allowing not only for a greater range of possibilities, but for a more individualistic expression. And we, as consumers, have reaped the benefits of this revolution in the wide array of choices and artistic tastes available to us.

Fine Flowers by Phone is a long-overdue guide to the best florists in the country. Its purpose is to provide a resource for

3

people who want high-quality flowers or arrangements delivered—across town or across the country—but are disillusioned with conventional wire services. This book tells you whom to call.

A ROSE IS NOT A ROSE IS NOT A ROSE: IDEAS AND ETIQUETTE

Once you've settled on a budget, the fun can begin: deciding just what kind of flower presentation you want to send. I use the word *presentation* instead of *bouquet* or *arrangement* because there are all sorts of other floral presents you can send besides a bouquet or an arrangement. Being a flower aficionado, I enjoy receiving any sort of gift related to flowers, as my friends well know, and many that I've received have been truly spectacular, and by no means ridiculously expensive—just thoughtful and clever.

After I spent several days "doing" flowers with Herb Plankinton, a fine florist from Delaware, Herb sent me six terra-cotta pots of paper-white narcissus, each pot tied off with a raffia knot and punctuated with curly willow. Not only was it chic, friendly and fragrant, but it was the kind of gift that's flexible. I could set the pots around the house as is (there's nothing more basic and handsome than terra-cotta, and it's compatible with any interior), replant the bulbs into another container, such as a large silver tureen, or simply drop the pots into decorative porcelain containers or baskets.

When I had my first child, a friend sent me a tiny terra-cotta pot of lilies of the valley, the dirt covered with "hump moss." It was small enough to keep next to my hospital bed, and fragrant enough without being noisome. The flower is exquisitely tiny, just like my daughter was, and conveys all the fresh associations of possibility one has with spring and a newborn baby.

There are a couple of guidelines you should bear in mind

when ordering floral gifts for someone in the hospital. Never send flowers that are highly fragrant, such as rubrum or white eratum lilies, gardenias, white freesias or paper-white narcissus. The sweet smell turns sickly very fast in a stuffy, hot hospital ward. Also, don't send flowers that need constant attention, such as cyclamen or hydrangeas. A drooping flower is outright depressing. Whatever you send to the hospital, keep it cheery. If you want to send a plant, orchids are great. They can take all kinds of abuse—for a period of time, anyway. The same advice goes for funerals: Go easy on the fragrance, and keep it cheery.

For a housewarming gift I once received a handsome dark gray metal pot inscribed with a shell motif and planted with a lady's slipper orchid. I could use the metal pot in the garden later, but for a month I had a lovely orchid. There's something reassuring about receiving flowers in the middle of a move. They remind you that there will be order and beauty, despite the fact that you are knee-deep in boxes and have kitchen paraphernalia all over the bedroom. They offer a glimpse of inspiring confidence.

One of my favorite stories is about a guest who wanted to send something memorable to his host and hostess to thank them for having had him to their country house for Labor Day weekend. The couple had recently bought the house, and dream plans for landscaping and decorating drifted in and out of their conversations. About a month later a peaceful, late-morning sleep was abruptly interrupted by four noisy workers in the yard. Dazed and confused, the couple ran out exclaiming there must be some mistake, soon to learn that their friend had ordered a thousand daffodils to be planted throughout the woods alongside the driveway. Now that's a very thoughtful gift. A less costly alternative to the same idea is a potted perennial that can be enjoyed indoors or on a porch while in bloom and then later planted in the garden.

A favorite beau of mine often brings me one perfect flower, exquisitely wrapped in clear cellophane and tied with a pretty ribbon. He's brought a daffodil, a garden rose, and a Casablanca lily. It's the perfect last-minute present, but not a good idea if you're going to somebody's house for dinner. On that occasion, always bring flowers in a container, because the last thing the host

5

or hostess wants to do is drop everything to see to your flowers. Your good intentions become an aggravating responsibility. In fact, if you want to give flowers, send them the day before with a card saying you're looking forward to the party. If it's a picnic or a pot-luck dinner, a basket of seasonal fruit with flowers is exciting. For Mother's Day last year, Eric Cogswell, a San Francisco designer, sent red tulips heaped with strawberries in a basket.

For children, I like to send something that's pretty and project-oriented. A bright red amaryllis planted with grass in a pot gives the child two things to watch: the spectacular unfolding of the blooms and the leggy green grass. Brightly colored baskets with multicolored flowers heaped with chocolate kisses is fun; a crate of herbs that the child can plant in the garden also makes a nice gift. To me, the last thing a youngster needs is another stuffed animal or leafy plant to catch dust. Inevitably the animal gets shoved in a closet, and the plant is neglected and dies a slow, discouraging death. Children need action and not too much responsibility!

Flowers in a combination with fruits and vegetables have saved the day as anniversary presents. For somebody's ruby fortieth, I heaped raspberries on coralbells, and when coral and jade were the call for a thirty-fifth, I arranged orange and green fruits in a basket with bunches of fragrant white freesias. I'll admit, I'm stumped for a solution to the fiftieth's gold requirements, because I refuse to paint flowers or foliage. However, these ideas must have started your imaginative wheels turning. Gifts of flowers can be tremendously varied; they can often be economical, and they send a message of thoughtfulness.

ARRANGEMENTS AND THEIR MOODS

When you ask for help from the fine florists described in this handbook, all kinds of creative answers are possible. Many of these florists do design special gifts for holidays and other occasions. But remember, you don't need to be clever all the time. There's often nothing better than a lovely bouquet of flowers or simply a dozen lilies or a profusion of field-grown zinnias.

When sending an arrangement, consider the feeling you want to convey. Cheery salutations are best expressed by lots of colors in a mixed bouquet. Weeds and meadow flowers are comfortable and warm, while all white is sophisticated and more formal. A small bouquet of white roses, freesias and paper-whites is wonderfully and tastefully romantic. Fortunately, our culture has not saddled flowers with all kinds of symbolic meaning, so we're pretty free to send what we want. A good florist is adept at expressing feelings with flowers, so communicate to him or her the emotion and occasion you're ordering for. Size, which is somewhat determined by budget, and color choices should always be stated, as well as the type of container.

FROM THE FLORIST'S POINT OF VIEW

If you call a florist with an unusual request, be considerate of the shopkeeper's schedule. He or she may have prior commitments to do seventy-five centerpieces for a rehearsal dinner that day and the wedding the next day. Florists are always overwhelmed during holiday seasons, especially Mother's Day. For Easter and Mother's Day, I always order my gifts two or three days ahead of time, before the crunch.

Sometimes florists become so overwhelmed during holidays, even when they've hired on extra staff, that they reach their capacity and have to stop taking orders. You may think this unprofessional, especially for a service business, but it is a realistic approach, and better than sending a bad arrangement or one that doesn't arrive at all. Quality and integrity are the florist's operational standards, as artistic vision is the lifeblood, and it takes only a short time for bad quality to destroy a reputation that may have taken years to build.

HOW MUCH WILL IT COST?

The most important consideration when placing an order for flowers, other than aesthetic preferences, is your budget. But how can you reconcile your imagined bouquet with your budget unless you know a few basics about why certain flowers cost more than others? Although pricing may appear random, there are a few basic facts that influence the price of flowers and the subsequent arrangement. First of all, the florist's prices are based upon the wholesaler's prices, whose prices, in turn, are subject to the grower's. These distribution channels coalesce to create the price structure. Other influences affecting the overall price structure may include seasonality, stem length, cultivation period, weather, popularity and holidays and variable operational costs, such as transportation, labor and currency fluctuations. The prices of certain imported flowers are greatly affected by currency fluctuations. When the dollar collapsed in 1988, for example, Dutch flowers, in comparison with those from Colombia or New Zealand, where the dollar was still strong, became prohibitively expensive.

SEASONALITY

As the market for greenhouse-grown flowers has become worldwide, wholesalers have begun to follow the sun around the globe to gather their inventory. When there isn't enough sunlight to grow tulips in greenhouses here, then wholesalers go to New Zealand (where our winter is their summer) for supplies, and so on down the line with the array of cut flowers that can be successfully cultivated in different parts of the world.

It might seem logical to think that if florists reaped their supplies from somewhere in the States, the flowers, no matter what the season, would be less expensive than those imported from faraway places like Holland, Israel or New Zealand. The effect of internationalization, however, has actually been to raise the local price structure, so the differences between imports and domestics has begun to disappear. Although seasonality does perceptibly influence the price of certain flowers, as internationalization expands to include more kinds of flowers the seasonal price curve for most greenhouse flowers will further flatten. Consequently, it is impossible to make any generalization about the seasonal effects on all flowers that are greenhouse-grown. Instead, you have to address the effects of seasonality on each flower, and the extent to which its cultivation has become "internationalized."

On the other hand, seasonality does have a considerable effect on the price of in-season field-grown flowers. When in season, field-grown orange and yellow lilies from Oregon cost less than imported ones. Locally grown annuals such as zinnias, bachelor's buttons and sunflowers purchased by a flower shop directly from local growers are significantly cheaper than those coming in from out of town. It's always a good idea to ask your florist what is in season *and* locally grown. Almost assuredly such flowers will be a good value. And a mass of zinnias is more fun to receive than a single orchid stem.

The one exception to this rule is that field-grown roses, whether hybrid or an old-fashioned variety, even when in season, are usually priced higher than their greenhouse counterparts, and certainly are more expensive than roses from South America. As growers perceive the increasing popularity of garden roses and begin producing more of them, this price differential is apt to shrink.

STEM LENGTH

Many flowers, such as roses, chrysanthemums, and tulips, come in various stem lengths. A general rule is that the longer the stem, the higher the price. The labor necessary to encourage these flowers to grow extra-long, phenomenally strong stems is expensive, and so they command a premium price. Consequently, a bunch (which is ten stems at the wholesale level) of long-stem tulips or roses is going to be pricier than the shorter version—usually by a lot. Since large arrangements inevitably require long-stem flowers, they can be expensive propositions. There are flowers with naturally long stems, such as white calla lilies, alstroemeria (Peruvian lily), certain hybrid delphiniums, liatris, *Campanula pyramidalis* and most tropicals. Since the price of these flowers does not vary according to stem length, an arrangement composed of them won't cost more for the added height.

CULTIVATION PERIOD

The cultivation period is the time it takes to grow a plant from a test-tube sliver or cutting to maturity; that is, to the point when it produces a supply of flowers worthy of being cut and shipped to market. How long this takes is reflected in the cost of the flower. Perennials such as coreopsis, the Shasta daisy, bee balm, salvia and yarrow all require a relatively short time—approximately two years for each plant to produce a healthy crop of flowers. On the other hand, peonies, garden roses and species iris need a considerably longer period. Hence the higher cost. Annual seed crops that have a sixty- to ninety-day turnaround period generally cost less than perennial crops. Examples of these annuals include zinnias, cosmos and petunias.

All blooming bushes and trees are relatively expensive, but they provide a considerably larger and longer-lasting look for the same amount of money you'd spend on cut flowers. Of course, some are more expensive than others. When you see a four-foot branch of dogwood in someone's living room, imagine how long it took a tree to produce that branch. Dogwoods probably grow about twelve inches a year. Conversely, bushes and trees that annually produce multiple suckers appropriate for cutting are less expensive. Examples include forsythia, quince, cherries, apples and magnolia. Cultivation period—along with supply and the cost of transportation—are the influences guiding the price of branches, whether they are used for springtime flowers or autumn color.

GROWERS' PERCEPTIONS: POPULARITY AND HOLIDAYS

When growers realize that a particular flower is easy to cultivate, relatively free of pests and a good cut flower (easy to ship and long-lived when placed in a vase), they begin to cultivate more and more of it. Inevitably the supply expands and the price drops. This has happened with alstroemeria and the gerbera daisy for example. A combination of grower participation and technological advances has brought the price of alstroemeria down by half over the last five years.

Growers' belief in the popularity of chrysanthemums, daisies and pompon carnations has caused the market to be flooded with these flowers. They are mass-produced in South America and Mexico, where there is an ample and cheap labor supply, good year-round temperature and intense sunlight. (You might wonder why Colombian growers don't raise tulips and other bulb flowers, thereby making them equally affordable, but in that climate the temperature extremes require too large an investment to create the right environment for bulb flowers such as those.) Americans importing from these countries have fared well in the face of currency fluctuations. The net effect of a huge supply, cheap labor, a good rate of exchange and favorable transportation costs is to make the price of most South and Central American flowers very competitive.

Nonetheless, a chart of the prices of individual flowers shows a dramatic increase in cost during holiday seasons, especially Valentine's Day. Most flowers double in price, some triple, from the month before till the month after a holiday. It's obvious that demand is up; another important factor, however, is the attention growers must bestow on their crops to get such a huge supply to mature perfectly for a specific date. In a sense, the higher prices are justified by the growers' timely efforts.

11

THE LANGUAGE OF *FINE FLOWERS BY PHONE*

Minimum Order. The stated minimums are for cut flower arrangements in vases only. The majority of these florists will send plants and wrap bouquets of loose cut flowers for less than the stated minimums.

Major Credit Cards. Includes American Express, Master-Card and VISA, although if you ask, some florists will accept other credit cards as well. When a shop does not accept all major credit cards, those that are accepted are indicated. "Credit to be arranged" means you and the florist will negotiate the terms of payment.

Best at Market. The florist has the option to substitute a choice of flowers determined by what he or she thinks is the best available alternative at market. For example, if you order a bunch of pink tulips and the available supply is damaged or old, the florist wants the right to substitute whatever he thinks is the most appropriate replacement given your budget and goals.

Free-lancer. A floral designer who works in a studio that is not accessible to the walk-in trade characteristic of retail shops. Because many free-lancers work on their own, some planning is required on your part. Most require twenty-four-hour notice and some even a week's notice. Most have answering machines.

Many free-lancers owned shops at one time during their careers, but chose the studio route for personal flexibility and professional focus. Before *Fine Flowers by Phone,* unless you knew a free-lancer by reputation there was no way to identify this talent. We are fortunate to have their participation in this book and their willingness to take on single gift orders, since most of their work is restricted to corporate accounts, parties and weddings. From time to time they, like some shops, will be unable to take your order if their time has already been booked. In most cases there is an alternative source in the specific city.

12

ALABAMA

BIRMINGHAM

The Flower Basket
LULA ROSE T. BLACKWELL

4228 Caldwell Mill Road
Birmingham, AL 35243
(205) 967-0777

If you grew up in the South as I did, with a reverence for anything romantic and larger than life, the name Lula Rose calls forth visions of Scarlett O'Hara and sweeping verandas draped with wisteria. Her work is as inspired as her reputation is grand. In the Constance Spry spirit, great strokes of style mass hundreds of stems of native foliage into huge fountains of flowers, spirited with a dash of wild abandon.

Important and sophisticated, an arrangement from Lula Rose evokes that larger-than-life vision that we occasionally glimpse . . . a momentary intuition of the sublime.

Minimum: $100.00
24-hour notice required
Credit to be arranged

Mountain Brook Flower Shop
MALOY LOVE

2407 Montevallo Road
Birmingham, AL 35223
(205) 870-1666

While taking care of third-generation customers, Maloy has stayed on top of the transition in styles. He has seen Christmas centerpieces of bowls of red carnations with variegated holly give way to oranges, cranberries, lilies and bear grass. While one arrangement looks like a slice of the garden, another may be a carefully conceived mosaic in the spirit of Fleur Cowles: lovely and romantic, but restrained and disciplined.

Maloy's goals are to please himself and the customer ... within limits. "I should be able to accommodate anybody within the realm of good taste," he claims. "I don't like anything artificial and despise abusing flowers for the sake of jokes—no 'forty and over the hill and here's a basket of dead flowers' kind of thing." His background is landscape architecture. Consequently he finds inspiration in art and nature. "And who knows which comes first?" he says. "I design with a committed spirit."

The shop is tiny, overflowing with carefully chosen flowers that are replenished three times a week. Maloy is dedicated to flowers and plants and does not fill the shelves with accessories or gift items. "Just one more thing to take care of. . . . We hardly have time to sweep the floor." In fact, customers are known to come in and pick up a broom—an admitted excuse to bask in the creative and friendly atmosphere that heightens the spirit. This is a special place.

Minimum: $25.00 plus delivery
All major credit cards

FLORENCE

The Added Touch
JOSEPHINE REDD AND PATTY JONES

445 Pallisade Drive
Florence, AL 35630
(205) 764-4304/-6013

Most small towns can't support a regular floral inventory of couture flowers such as Casablanca lilies or even dozens of tulips in the off-season, but such practical matters don't preclude an appreciation of the aesthetic at The Added Touch. When Josephine's and Patty's talents tackle the flora of their geographic location—the flowers and foliage coming straight from the yard and local gardens—the results are magnificent. Which is not to say that imports are not available with sufficient notice.

Nevertheless, what do you send in the dead of winter? The Added Touch recommends a basket of planted material or a clever display of massed carnations all cut the same length and tied off with a lead bow. The aesthetic is alive and flourishing in Florence!

Minimum: $50.00 plus delivery
Credit cards: MasterCard and VISA
Also serves: Killen, Muscle Shoals, Russellville, Sheffield and Tuscumbia

HUNTSVILLE

Caroline Noojin
CAROLINE NOOJIN

1104 Deborah Drive
Huntsville, AL 35801
(205) 883-0558

English-style arrangements with a romantic southern accent flourish here. Caroline excels in loose and airy combinations of imported, wild or garden flowers, sometimes combining them with fruit. Rubrum lilies with nectarines, plums, grapes and apples cascade over silver baskets. Cranberry, crape myrtle, minicarnations, peegee hydrangeas and garden roses are punctuated by blooming wildflowers. Potted plants such as violets and ivies tied with ribbons drape over the edge of a carefully chosen basket. "People seem to want their flowers to have that natural look these days, and it's to that desire that I cater." And indeed she succeeds.

Minimum: $40.00 plus delivery
48-hour notice required
Credit to be arranged
Also serves: Decatur

MOBILE

Zimlich Brothers Florist & Greenhouses, Inc.
RON BARRETT AND THE ZIMLICH FAMILY

7700 Airport Boulevard
Mobile, AL 36608
(205) 639-0107

The typical Ron Barrett arrangement looks as if fresh blooms, foliage and wild grasses had been collected from the fields and woods all afternoon. There is no end to the selection of materials used to create these bouquets. Customers in the Zimlich stores are very aggressive and up-to-date on the current world flower markets. The effect demands a closer look. The natural designs show off deep interior studies of tiny select blooms and mosses. This "inside treat" has become a trademark of Ron's arrangements.

Ron has been in business with the Zimlich family for twelve years and spends most of his time handling the special events— weddings, bar mitzvahs and Mardi Gras balls; however, he also keeps a close eye on the quality of the day-to-day work. Nevertheless, keep your plans simple and specific to avoid being lost in Zimlich's commercial maze.

Minimum: $30.00 plus delivery
All major credit cards
Also serves: Axis, Fairhope, Saraland, Satsuma, Semmes, Theodore and Tilmans Corner

SHEFFIELD

Lola's Gifts and Flowers
CARL CASIDAY

214 North Montgomery Avenue
Sheffield, AL 35660
(205) 383-2299

The tone here is woodsy, wild and wonderful. Carl dramatically combines dried roses, twigs, grapevines and hydrangeas in overscaled, mass arrangements, yet he's certainly capable of being traditional if the occasion calls for something more subdued. When he takes advantage of native materials and unendangered wildflowers in a mix with his Holland imports, the results are always restrained and sophisticated.

Last Mother's Day, Carl combined in a rustic, natural vine basket everything the color or smell of peach: potpourri, ribbon, gerberas and tulips, accented with a little Queen Anne's lace and heightened with peach-blossom twigs. Any mom on the receiving end got the implied, warm salutation—"You're peachy."

Carl goes on the road frequently, giving lectures and demonstrations. This usually is a red flag to me: If the owner is often gone, then how can we be assured that day-to-day quality is going to be up to standard? Carl is fortunate to have family members who work with him . . . and so are we. If you ever get the chance to hear him give a talk, it's a treat.

Minimum: $20.00 plus delivery
All major credit cards
Also serves: Florence, Muscle Shoals, and Tuscumbia

TUSCALOOSA

Phillip's Crimson Gardens
PHILLIP WALES

1902 Hackberry Lane
Tuscaloosa, AL 35401
(205) 758-0483

In an old brick house on a shaded lane, Phillip and his family have set up their shop to display the tasteful ways to enjoy flowers on a daily basis. The fireplace mantel is always decorated according to the season, hanging plants adorn the corners, and flowers are scattered throughout the room.

Phillip's arrangements are natural and easy. Distinctive branches and greens, such as quince, crab apple or euonymus are combined with flowers imported from all over the world: tulips, freesias, rubrum lilies and lilac. "My goal is to enjoy doing what I do and sharing that with others. I won't do anything that I wouldn't want for myself. I am known to turn away business that I think would reflect badly on me as well as on the customer." That's a tough standard to maintain in a small city, but it's the sign of a great florist, one who will not be just anything to everybody.

Minimum: $25.00 plus delivery
Credit cards: MasterCard and VISA
Also serves: Northport

ARIZONA

PHOENIX

Brady's Interior Design & Florist
RON AND TERRY BRADY

4167 North Marshall Way
Scottsdale, AZ 85251
(602) 945-8776

In a phrase, this is the big time—
however, there is no lack of attention to detail. It's rare that a shop can brilliantly conceive and execute fabulous parties all over the country and at the same time ensure that gift arrangements go out with similar integrity. The Bradys' style is loose and airy, using imported flowers such as lilies, roses, delphiniums and tulips. Ninety percent of all their containers are made in-house: mossed oasis, glass bowls trimmed with lead bows and glass vases wrapped in hand-painted fabrics and tied off with silk cording.

Looking back over fourteen years of business, Terry says, "We have always challenged ourselves. Arranging flowers in a vase or just doing the centerpieces for a party is not enough. We carefully consider every detail from original conception of the idea to the presentation. Every element is important to us."

Minimum: $40.00 plus delivery
All major credit cards

TUCSON

The Plantsman
RON MCBAIN

3302 North Country Club
Tucson, AZ 85716
(602) 795-4130

Ron's style is English but with a Flemish cast. His very full arrangements include lots of Holland imports combined with the flowers he grows himself. "My favorite way to start the day is to wake up very early and pick all the best flowers from the garden." Wonderful European baskets are brimming with choice flowers such as lily of the valley, muscari and unusual orchids and punctuated with dramatic branches of forsythia, quince, cherry, birch or curly willow, among others. It's this kind of thorough dedication that makes The Plantsman such a special shop and any gift from here a delight.

Ron's talents extend to contemporary, high-style arrangements as well.

Minimum: $25.00 plus delivery
All major credit cards
Also serves: Surrounding suburbs

ARKANSAS

HOT SPRINGS

House of Flowers
JEAN MILLER AND IRIS SWANEY

111 Hollywood Lane
Hot Springs, AR 71901
(501) 623-1351

Four generations of this family have arranged flowers here, creating everything from traditional funeral work to floral horse blankets for the Oaklawn racetrack. The range of styles is as diverse as the occasions they design for. Flowers are shipped in from all over the world, while seasonal garden flowers are chosen from a selection of local sources. "Even in winter, we cut a lot of our greens locally," says Mrs. Miller. "I think our local pine, cedar and magnolia are far superior to what we can order from out of town." A narrow selection of tropicals is always on hand, but anything can be ordered. Daily arrangements go out in baskets or clear glass.

Another member of the family owns an extensive greenhouse operation and keeps the shop filled with foliage and blooming plants as well as herbs. The list is extensive, including bougainvillea, ferns, bromeliads, begonias, tulips and daffodils, but you should restrict your scope to seasonal choices.

There is a large range of materials and talent here, so be sure to be specific about what you do and don't want.

Minimum: $20.00 plus delivery
Credit cards: MasterCard and VISA

LITTLE ROCK

Petals
LEA ANNE BUMPERS

400 North Bowman Suite 8A
Little Rock, AR 72212
(501) 224-3334

Tropicals and Holland imports abound in this tiny shop, but on a day-to-day basis Lea Anne's arrangements achieve a wispy, straight-from-the-meadow look. She accomplishes this by using dramatic and unusual filler flowers. Instead of the traditional baby's breath and tiny mums, she reaches for the unexpected—summer aster, white wax and locap—and combines these with big, important flowers.

At Christmas, pomegranates and purple grapes spill out of Italian terra-cotta containers. "I use anything that's deep red to purple," Lea Anne says. "And I mix it with pheasant feathers, greens and tapestry ribbons." When Christmas arrangements are done in glass bowls, the bowls are wrapped in tapestry fabrics. The look is rich, handsome and always classic.

Lea Anne creates lovely potpourri baskets, decorated with dried and silk flowers. Fresh flowers are incorporated as well. There are endless ideas here—I've only scratched the surface.

Minimum: $17.50 plus delivery
All major credit cards

Phil Cato
PHIL CATO

5413 C Street
Little Rock, AR 72205
(501) 666-2769

Phil cultivates five acres of field-grown flowers, all to be cut and used in his floral work.

"Without this, I couldn't do what I do," he explains. What Phil does are spectacular natural bouquets that dazzle the eye with their energy. His arrangements incorporate old-fashioned flowers, such as hollyhock, rudbeckia, black-eyed Susan, roses and Queen Anne's lace, with all kinds of herbs, vegetables and fruits, either on or off the vine. Phil will also incorporate wild blackberry, huckleberry or raspberry sprigs and the branches of flowering trees and bushes into his arrangements. "During the growing season, everything I use is from the field or the countryside. Of course, during the colder months, I must import my flowers."

During the winter, to add to his imported flowers Phil takes advantage of the local fauna, using pheasant or quail feathers and even turkey tails for an added touch. He has access to wonderful herbs and flowering topiaries as well. Daily arrangements go out in your choice of either a basket or a clear glass container.

Minimum: $50.00 plus delivery
24-hour notice required
Credit to be arranged

PINE BLUFF

Wade Black Florist
EARL VICK

909 Cherry Street
Pine Bluff, AR 71601
(501) 536-2200

Mr. Vick's talents allow him to be daring and original, but his first goal is to please his customer. He carries lots of Dutch flowers, blooming plants and foliages, as well as spectacular locally grown orchids. He doesn't carry tropicals on a daily basis, but with notice he can get them.

You'll be asked many specific questions, so give specific answers. If you find floral jargon confusing, though, you might want to stick to a basket of blooming plants or simply a bunch of whatever's freshest: roses from his Ocalona grower, white carnations, or zinnias massed in a clear glass container.

Minimum: $25.00 plus delivery
Credit cards: MasterCard and VISA

CALIFORNIA

BAKERSFIELD

The Garden District
TOM HEATH AND SHERYL CHURCHWELL

8200 Stockdale Highway, Suite H-1
Bakersfield, CA 93311
(805) 834-9200

"There's nothing I can't do, and no one can outdo what I do, but there are things I won't do—like spray-paint flowers and foliages. Whatever end of the design spectrum that I'm working in, from high-style to traditional, my first priority includes respecting the flowers and pleasing the customer," explains Tom. "I believe it's a real accomplishment to be creative and get paid for it!"

Fresh flowers from all over the world take center stage in this slick shop. Its strongly architectural look, dotted with glass-block display stands and skylights, is inviting. Attractive containers range from handsome baskets to terra-cotta vases with teal blue handles, to lots of clear glass. Tom's blooming plants and orchids inspire the imagination, suggesting wonderful combinations for planted baskets. In-house specials are designed for holidays, so be sure to ask. Otherwise, be specific about what you want and your order will be well taken care of.

Minimum: $35.00 plus delivery
All major credit cards
Also serves: Oildale

BEL AIR

Solarium . . . More Than a Florist
MARC LOWY

The Glen Center
2922 Beverly Glen Circle
Bel Air, CA 90077
(213) 475-0401

T his is the best of Hollywood and
Beverly Hills rolled into one. Huge arrangements of roses, lilies,
delphiniums and tropicals are set off by lavish, exotic foliage. When
appropriate, Marc and his associates are known to incorporate
grand strokes of glitter stick. The work here is big, important and
unrestrained glitz.

When I was in the shop, they had an eclectic selection of
gifts, from mirrored hand vases to urns inspired by neoclassicism.
There are many wonderful orchid plants, too.

Minimum: $30.00 plus delivery
All major credit cards

BERKELEY

Carrie Wright
CARRIE WRIGHT

2218½ Los Angeles Avenue
Berkeley, CA 94707
(415) 524-9820

A lthough Carrie uses what are
broadly termed cottage-garden flowers (many of which are specially

grown for her so she can get just the look she wants), her work is far from cute or quaint. Her style is to use a profusion of garden flowers arranged in surprising splendor. Her skills imbue wild, grassy, weedlike flowers with importance and grandeur. If you've ever been to Alice Water's restaurant, Chez Panisse, then you've seen Carrie's spirited arrangements.

Minimum: $50.00 plus delivery
3 days' notice required
All major credit cards
Also serves: Oakland and Piedmont

BEVERLY HILLS

Flourish and Garlande, Ltd.
JULIE A. CHAPMAN, AIFD, AND JOY MYERSCOUGH

9040 Burton Way
Beverly Hills, CA 90211
(213) 271-5030

Julie and Joy find their inspiration in historical, picturesque Flemish and Edwardian bouquets. Many dedicated growers throughout California keep this shop supplied with special perennials, wildflowers and herbs that the proprietors combine with their Dutch and French imports. Tulips, lilies, scented geraniums and fennel are mixed with a deft though casual abandon. Presentations range in mood and style from free-spirited country to romantic and dreamy. Tropicals are not always stocked but can be special-ordered.

The shop is well supplied with antique containers from France, Italy and England, as well as with glass containers and modern-day baskets made from material of all sorts, from twigs to herbs. A popular request here is a topiary tree made from flowers, dried in-house, in colors to match the room they are intended for. Sizes range from six inches in height to six feet.

Minimum: $25.00 plus delivery
All major credit cards

BURLINGAME

Gardenhouse
BRUCE AND MARSHA ATKINSON

1129 Howard Avenue
Burlingame, CA 94010
(415) 347-2967

Marsha describes her work as "English and timeless." One of her arrangements might be a robust combination of garden roses, delphinium, lilac, stock, variegated pittosporum and grapevine cascading over the edges of a full vase, filling any room with its subtle fragrance.

While Bruce and Marsha's arrangements are breathtaking, the range of decorative accessories at the Gardenhouse is exciting: jardinieres of lavender; fabulous dried flowers and foliages for topiaries and baskets; custom Versailles boxes; wooden crates with copper handles for an herb collection or a mass of spring bulbs; French ribbons; lead containers from England; croquet mallets from Australia; handsome terra-cotta containers; baskets; and glass vases. This shop speaks of a life-style that's both comfortable and complete, with an inspired aesthetic discipline.

Minimum: $35.00 plus delivery
24-hour notice required
Credit cards: MasterCard and VISA
Also serves: Hillsborough and San Mateo

CARMEL

Flowers Ltd.
ANNE PATRICK AND ROB REINKENS

P.O. Box 1108
Carmel, CA 93953
(408) 625-2404

A native of England, Anne was chief demonstrator and decorator at the Constance Spry School for twenty years. Ten years ago she married a fellow floral designer, moved to Carmel and opened this shop.

Anne finds her inspiration in the garden: Her arrangements are a full, lush mix of garden flowers that come directly from local growers, who also supply the shop with interesting foliages. "We have one grower who has three hundred varieties of daffodils and supplies us with them almost year round," says Rob. Tropicals are imported from Hawaii and New Zealand to round out the selection.

Anne and Rob create lots of lovely planted baskets full of blooming plants, orchids and foliages. Special gift ideas are developed for holidays. Last Valentine's Day, for example, hearts of dried roses and swatches of old lace were incorporated into arrangements and planted baskets. There are proprietary gift items as well: painted baskets, usually in vertigris or white with matching steel bows, and specially made Versailles boxes that you can order in many colors and in sizes from six inches on up.

Arrangements go out in glass, baskets or terra-cotta containers. If you order a European wrap bouquet, it's wrapped in cello and tied off with ribbons.

Minimum: $25.00 plus delivery
All major credit cards
Also serves: Carmel Valley, Pacific Grove and Pebble Beach

Tutto Bella
JIM ("J.D.") HINTON
1805C Contra Costa
Sand City, CA 93955
(408) 899-5644

Jim, known as J.D. to people in the Bay area, ventured out to the West Coast after years of working with merchandise display and flower design at Neiman-Marcus in Dallas. He then traveled the country for three years, opening various stores for Ralph Lauren and arranging their flowers and plants. Finally, in the fall of 1983, he moved to Carmel and started Tutto Bella. Then all of 265 square feet, it's now been expanded to 15,000. J.D. saw a floral vacuum to be filled. His goals are to create arrangements with flair and good design rather than the typical "round mound" look often associated with many wire services.

J.D. is well known in the area. He and his staff can create anything, from the most exotic arrangements to simply beautiful country-garden baskets. You can give J.D. a context, let him do what he wants and relax—it will be fabulous.

Topiaries are also a specialty.

Minimum: $30.00 plus delivery
Credit cards: MasterCard and VISA
Also serves: Carmel Valley, Monterey and Pebble Beach

HOLLYWOOD

William Carl Alspaugh and Associates
WILLIAM C. ALSPAUGH

838 North Las Palmas Avenue
Hollywood, CA 90038
(213) 465-2772

A free-lancer now, William was formerly assistant to David Jones, where he became well known not only for his brilliant work but also for the way he answered the phone: "William for David." He subsequently opened his own retail shop and called it William for William. After owning the store for a while, he concluded he could not maintain quality rapport with his clients because of the distractions inherent in running a retail operation. It's clear that William loves his flowers and his clients and doesn't want anything to interfere with those dynamics. For him, free-lancing is the only answer.

He describes his work as "lots of garden-fresh flowers in not a lot of space." For gifts, he likes to send hand-tied bouquets wrapped in clear cellophane, in the English tradition.

Minimum: $50.00 plus delivery
24-hour notice required
Best at market
Credit to be arranged

LAGUNA BEACH

Cliff Fulkerson
CLIFF FULKERSON

1199 South Coast Highway
Laguna Beach, CA 92651
(714) 494-7114

T his shop is located in a two-story Tudor building with an ocean view and a fine collection of nineteenth-century English and French antiques. Here Cliff creates one dramatic arrangement after another for clients as far away as Monte Carlo and as close as right down the street. "I have a whole truckload of dried-flower topiaries to be picked up for a wedding in Saudi Arabia," he says. Indeed, Cliff has a reputation that travels well.

"A detail we're known for when appropriate is tying off our

arrangements with ribbon or raffia and gluing a pearl in the center of the knot or bow."

Minimum: $25.00 plus delivery
All major credit cards
Also serves: Corona del Mar, Dana Point, Laguna Hills, Laguna Niguel, Newport Beach and San Clemente

Miles–Randolph, Inc.
RANDY HARMER, AIFD, AND SHIRLEY MILES

22732 Granite Way, Suite C
Laguna Hills, CA 92653
(714) 951-9680

Randy Harmer's soft-spoken manner belies his prominence in the industry. He's extremely well liked by his peers and clients, and his talents are viewed with deep respect. From his ten-thousand-square-foot studio, brimming over with thousands of flowers both locally grown and imported, Randy and his talented staff oversee the weekly floral and foliage installations for numerous hotels such as the Ritz Carlton in Laguna Beach and the Four Seasons in Newport Beach. Despite their many corporate accounts, they give their full personal attention to social events and daily gift orders.

With such a diverse clientele, they're adept at many styles, ranging from strong-line contemporary creations influenced by Oriental design, to grand tapestry-like displays in the Flemish tradition. No detail is overlooked and every arrangement, even a simple selection of flowers, is exquisitely presented. A dozen Casablanca lilies slipped into a clear glass cylinder filled with red cranberries and tied off with gold cording is elegant and sophisticated and a perfect example of Randy's talent.

Minimum: $35.00 plus delivery
All major credit cards
Also serves: Anaheim, Costa Mesa, Dana Point, El Toro, Irvine,

Laguna Niguel, Mission Viejo, Newport Beach, San Clemente and Santa Ana

LOS ANGELES

See also Bel Air, Beverly Hills, Hollywood, Malibu, Pacific Palisades, Pasadena and West Hollywood

Milo Bixby, Inc.
MILO BIXBY

545 South Figueroa
Los Angeles, CA 90071
(213) 622-8184

The same talent that makes Milo's store in San Marino such a success is also evident here. For more information, see the write-up on Milo Bixby, Inc., under San Marino.

Bloomsbury Floral Design
HAL SPRAGG AND JEFF WHITE

P.O. Box 481267
Los Angeles, CA 90048
(213) 855-1001

There's a simple approach to design here: Flowers are stem length and combined as they're found in nature. Hal and Jeff prefer to keep tropicals and garden flowers in separate arrangements. This approach system serves as a backdrop to endless and exciting creativity, particularly regarding gifts. Wooden crates in the rough, washed with colored stains or painted in a Cézannesque style may be filled with organically grown herbs.

Given 24-hour notice, the shopkeepers will collect some of the finest and freshest baby vegetables and fruits, combining them with flowers for a new approach to the old—and often unappetizing—fruit-basket idea. European-style bouquets are wrapped with complimentary tissue, cellophane and ribbons. Specially made vases, from contemporary to neoclassic to quaint, are available. Innovative and tasteful.

Minimum: $35.00 plus delivery
All major credit cards

Campo dei Fiori
ROBIN ANN FARRELL AND SIMONA ENNAS

648 Martel (at Melrose)
Los Angeles, CA 90036
(213) 655-9966

The proprietors of Campo dei Fiori give their work an exotic look that some people don't understand. It's not unusual for them to take an heliconia leaf or a banana leaf and cut it, "you know, to give it some shape," says Ms. Ennas. "We have gotten calls complaining about sending old leaves, but after giving an explanation, the arrangement, seen through newly educated eyes, evokes exclamatory raves that won't stop." Although they can do anything, their talents are given to voluminous, asymmetrical arrangements using tropicals, with strong overtones of ikebana.

Ask about the strikingly handsome gray, black or white vases that are made exclusively for Campo dei Fiori from a cement and plastic amalgam.

Minimum: $35.00 plus delivery
All major credit cards

David Jones
DAVID JONES

Showroom: 8591 Sunset Boulevard
Los Angeles, CA 90069
(213) 659-6347

Offices and studio: Gene Mulligan
5790 West Washington Boulevard
Culver City, CA 90230
(213) 934-8311

David Jones has been shaping tastes and styles for thirty years. He is one of the few outside florists asked to decorate the entire White House. A list of David's customers could serve as a guide to where the movers and shakers party.

His style can be summed up in the phrase expensive simplicity. One of his most popular floral gifts consists of four terracotta pots of amaryllis, whose blossoms are the size of dinner plates. David does grand arrangements, too—he designed the flowers for Adam's wedding on television's "Dynasty."

Minimum: $40.00 plus delivery
Credit cards: MasterCard and VISA

LOS GATOS

Nature's Alley
JAN AND DAVE BREES

108 Santa Cruz Avenue
Los Gatos, CA 95030
(408) 354-4221

There are no cut flowers at Nature's Alley. Rustic baskets and decorative pots hold a selection of live foliage and blooming plants that can be used both in- and outdoors. On close inspection, there is a perceptible variety in Jan and Dave's various planted compositions. A presentation can be very sophisticated or, as they say, "personal, warm and a bit fuzzy; but there is nothing cutsy or craftsy about it." There is integrity in every design, and refinement of detail: Hand-painted birds, birds' nests and French ribbons abound. Often the baskets are accented with lead or copper bows, knots or simple trimming.

"What's really exciting and challenging in my very specialized business is all the new types of bulbs and plants that are just beginning to come into this country from South Africa and New Zealand," says Ms. Brees.

Minimum: $25.00 plus delivery
Credit cards: MasterCard and VISA
Also serves: Atherton, Cupertino, Mountain View, Palo Alto, Portola Valley, Sunnyvale and Woodside

MALIBU

Renato
RENATO SEIZA

21337 Pacific Coast Highway
Malibu, CA 90265
(213) 456-3636

Like the other Los Angeles–area florists in this book, Renato has a long list of stars to whom he caters. His style is contemporary, blending native grasses like pampas or bear grass with southwestern succulents like hen and chickens or sedums. It's high style with a southwestern twist in strong-line compositions.

Minimum: $25.00 plus delivery
All major credit cards

MODESTO

The Thoughtful Flower
MICHAEL MERRITT

429 McHenry Avenue
Modesto, CA 95354
(209) 521-1451

Michael's arrangements are full and vibrant whether he's creating a strong-line arrangement or a massed bouquet. His distinctive style consistently shows off his talent for flowers and his good taste. His flowers are both locally grown and imported, and he uses a challenging variety of flowering vines, grasses, foliage and flowers, many of which a lot of us have never seen before. We all know what bromeliads are, for example, but how many of us have seen them with small pendent bracts of yellow and orange?

Michael has a unique flair for depth and detail and a special talent for combining wildflowers with exotic ones. An arrangement of oranges and yellows combines kangaroo paws and oncidium orchids with native grasses, wild mustard, poppies, freesias, lilies and salmon-colored tulips. Or wild oats rain down, glistening, on a collection of white flowers, including Easter lilies, amaryllis and tulips. Every presentation invites repeated study, for each one reveals something new, a flower or some foliage you didn't see the last time you looked. With a master stroke, all these little parts combine to produce a melodic and pleasing whole.

Michael is one of the most talented florists around, so whatever your plans are here, leave as much as possible to his discretion, including the container. His inventory of vases is as varied, interesting and attractive as his flowers and foliage.

Minimum: $35.00 plus delivery
All major credit cards
Also serves: Ceres, Escalon, Ripon and Riverbank

NOVATO

Morning Glory Flowers
PURU PANDEY

1721 Grant Avenue
Novato, CA 94945
(415) 897-8964

It's a special case when I call attention to a particular designer in a shop. I do so only when the designer, in conjunction with the owner, is setting the standards. At Morning Glory Flowers, everything Natalie Foster and Peru do is naturally beautiful. Natalie makes the prettiest hand-tied bouquets I've ever seen—reminiscent of the bouquets in the magazine ads for Estée Lauder perfume. They recall dreams dripping with romance.

Minimum: $22.00 plus delivery
All major credit cards
Also serves: Corte Madera, Fairfax, Ignacio, Larkspur, Mill Valley, San Rafael, Sausalito, Terra Linda and Tiburon

OAKLAND

Bloomies
ILONA BERTA AND MICHELA MAIDEN

Rockridge Market Mall
5655 College Avenue
Oakland, CA 94618
(415) 547-0444

If you didn't know any better, you'd think Bloomies is just a bucket shop—pick out your cut

37

flowers, pay for them and leave. But behind this chic market facade lurks wonderful talents. My advice is to take advantage of them, and you'll be pleasantly surprised by the crisp and colorful romantic creations.

Minimum: $35.00 plus delivery
Credit cards: MasterCard and VISA
Also serves: Alameda, Albany, Berkeley, Emeryville, Kensington, Orinda, Piedmont and Walnut Creek

ONTARIO

Roger's Flower Shop
MAURICE CRAIG

413 North Euclid
Ontario, CA 91762
(714) 986-6207

A native Californian, Maurice bought his flower shop from Roger in 1944 and never changed the name. You can be sure he knows his customers and the local needs, but when he doesn't, he's quick to ask preferences. His look is primarily English inspired, but Maurice believes he's in an area where one can't be limited to one specific design style. His work ranges from an open, loose look incorporating garden-type flowers and branches that go out in glass containers, baskets, terra-cotta pots or wooden crates, to dramatic, contemporary, high-style arrangements.

All of his flowers are bought at market since he has no dedicated growers to rely on. The shop is filled with assorted blooming plants and orchids, which he draws on for his planted baskets. Special gift ideas are created for holidays. Last Mother's Day, for example, Country Dairy lotions and bath salts were incorporated into European bouquets and planted baskets. Be sure to ask what's on the holiday menu, if that's when you're calling.

Minimum: $20.00 plus delivery
All major credit cards
Also serves: Chino, Claremont, Montclair, Pomona, Rancho Cucamonga and Upland

PACIFIC PALISADES

The Beverly Hills Flower Express
ROBERT LANE AND TOM BURNHAM

15117 Sunset Boulevard
Pacific Palisades, CA 90272
(213) 454-1334

"There is nothing tortured in this shop. We don't bend it, mold it or mutilate it. . . . Instead, we have great respect for the natural shape and fall of each flower and foliage," says Mr. Burnham. The Robert Lane approach is the artistic juxtaposition of unexpected materials, for which he has hundreds of sources. "Twice a year we get a truckload of unusual branches from a tree collector outside of San Diego after he prunes his trees. And we get mosses, mushrooms and lichens from a farmer in Oregon."

Robert is also known for his clever holiday creations. And his planted baskets are simply voluptuous—Rubenesque. His parties are the toast of LA, a town that's hard to impress. There's a lot of depth as well as style here.

Minimum: $50.00 plus delivery
All major credit cards

PALM DESERT

Comerford's
JEANNE COMERFORD

73890 El Paseo
Palm Desert, CA 92260
(619) 568-3587

English-garden arrangements and French-style bouquets are the custom here, but tropicals can be had on request. The shop reflects this taste, filled with English and French antiques as well as handsome glass, fine porcelains and reproduction Williamsburg pieces.

In a desert where aficionados have rightfully had laws passed imposing heavy fines for picking any flora, all flowers are bought at market or imported. Comerford's is mindful of the desert's dry heat by choosing greens and flowers that do well in these extreme conditions. It has a special field-grown ivy for its planted baskets, which incorporate branches and cut flowers amongst the ivy, flowering plants and other green plants. The shop is known for its unusual and creative arrangements. Thus—like most of the florists in this handbook—it provides flowers for some of the area's finest homes, restaurants, hotels and country clubs.

Minimum: $25.00 plus delivery
Credit cards: MasterCard and VISA
Also serves: Cathedral City, Indian Wells, Indio, La Quinta, Rancho Mirage and Palm Springs

PASADENA

Silver Birches
WALTER HUBERT

180 East California Boulevard
Pasadena, CA 91005
(818) 796-1431

Like others in the floral business, Walter has expanded his shop to include interior and landscape design, with a specialty in flower borders and cutting gardens as well as vegetable and herb gardens. This transition has strengthened Silver Birches' floral department, and Walter has been fortunate in hiring several designers on whom he can rely to maintain his standards.

Walter and his associates strive to present flowers as naturally as possible. One of their innovative techniques is to soak sea-grape leaves or melaleuca bark until pliable, and then wrap it around either a flowerpot or a vase. Once it hardens, the arrangement looks as though it's actually growing. Walter says, "Such treatment even dignifies that old standby, the gloxinia, and the pot becomes affordable sculpture. We're not afraid to try something new, and we always hope that people will like it."

Many ideas from both the landscaping and the interior business are creatively carried over into the flower shop. For example, Silver Birches is well known for its appealing display of practical herbs in weathered wooden crates, just the right size for keeping outdoors but easily carried inside when desired. Not only are they useful, but they make wonderful centerpieces. There are many unique ideas here, so ask.

Careful consideration is given to the presentation of gift arrangements. Beautiful stationery is inscribed with calligraphy. If something is to be wrapped, hat pins are used, never staples. At Silver Birches, they believe the actual receiving of flowers should be as much an event as the occasion for sending them.

41

Minimum: $25.00 plus delivery
All major credit cards

PIEDMONT

Ron Morgan
RON MORGAN

342 Highland Avenue
Piedmont, CA 94611
(415) 655-0321

Ron Morgan has been defining floral standards for his discriminating East Bay clientele for years. His versatile talents, punctuated with a tasteful pizzazz, have an undeniable aesthetic influence on all the goings-on about Piedmont. His vibrant personality and *joie de vivre* are reflected in all his work, whether it's a strong-line contemporary arrangement or a large, luscious romantic bouquet.

His large shop is filled with an eclectic gift assortment, from the latest designs in dried topiaries to the newest potpourri; terracotta, ironstone and clear glass containers are also available, as are baskets. Ron even carries a selection of botanical prints.

Since Piedmont is such a gardener's Eden, everyone's garden is filled with flowers ready for cutting. Ron is astutely aware of this and stocks his flowers to order. To be assured of freshness and variety, he recommends you place your order two to three days in advance. Give him your choice of container and style of bouquet, then relax; your order will be masterfully executed.

Minimum: $30.00 plus delivery
All major credit cards
Also serves: Alameda, Albany, Berkeley, Contra Costa County, Emeryville, Kensington, Oakland, Orinda and Santa Clara

REDLANDS

Derrick & Co., A Florist
DERRICK VASQUEZ, AIFD, AND MICHAEL LOPEZ

218 Orange Street
Redlands, CA 92373
(714) 792-2939

Arrangements from Derrick & Co. are lush and lovely, romantic and soothing. Although they are capable of anything, Derrick and Michael prefer working in the European style, covering the relatively specialized spectrum from Renaissance della Robbia to full Victorian bouquets, grand English arrangements and French country baskets. French ribbons and raffia are often incorporated into their work, but not as the expected bows; instead you'll find surprising treatments such as winding French knots that march down the stems of a Victorian bouquet, or swaths of raffia braided down the trunk of a stunning white azalea. Everything is dramatically and tastefully executed, even within the limitations made necessary by the heat of this California valley: "We are restricted from using extremely fragile flowers such as iris or lily of the valley," says Derrick. "We want our flowers to last."

Their shop is a cornucopia of imaginative surprises: Renaissance garlands drape a table set for afternoon tea; pomegranate and rose topiaries stand on a gilt entrance table below a collection of botanical prints; packages of decorative, fragrant potpourri spill out of antique papier-mâché trunks.

A tempting selection of vases includes hand-blown glass, lots of terra-cotta, some with *faux* finishes, and handsome baskets. They carry gourmet truffles, the complete Crabtree & Evelyn line of foods and soaps, and Paperwhite linens and laces. It's the kind of shop you can spend hours looking around and still not see everything, but you'll surely be inspired by the talent.

43

Minimum: $25.00 plus delivery
All major credit cards
Also serves: San Bernardino and surrounding area

SACRAMENTO

Impressions
TERRE PENROD ROTH

3050 Fite Cirlce, Suite 113
Sacramento, CA 95827
(916) 636-2003

Terre Roth moved to Sacramento from southeastern Missouri, bringing with her a strong belief in value, quality and personal service. Sacramento seems to have accepted her enthusiasm with eagerness and gratitude. Her early training there was as the manager of a contemporary high-style shop. She followed this by opening her own free-lance studio, which she maintained full-time for "just two short, exciting years."

Terre opened her retail shop last year but will keep the studio to create arrangements for weddings and large parties. She says, "My designers and I can design anything, from lovely, soft and natural English-garden arrangements to unusual tropicals to unique contemporaries, electric and daring. But our real flair is creating moods and responses in floral art form, translating a client's desires into reality and, in the process, finding our own expression."

Minimum: $30.00 plus delivery
All major credit cards
Also serves: Cameron Park, El Dorado Hills, Elk Grove, Rancho Cordova, Rancho Murieta and Roseville

SAINT HELENA

Florabunda
LELAIN CRIST

P.O. Box 515
St. Helena, CA 94574
(707) 963-1128

Lelain is one of those inspired florists who see the aesthetic possibilities in what most of us would discard as weeds. From the roadside and meadows she gathers wonderful grasses and flowers and combines them loosely with her garden flowers and Holland imports in a natural country style. "I try not to put things together that you wouldn't normally see in nature," she says. "For instance, if I am doing something with garden roses I like to put wild-rose foliage with it." Lelain's work is seasonal, and she's in the business "to celebrate the passage of the seasons and share that joy with other people."

Her arrangements are in terra-cotta pots or baskets and, when she can get them, bird's nests.

Minimum: $25.00 plus delivery within a 15-mile radius
Credit to be arranged
Also serves: Calistoga, Napa, Rutherford and Yountville

SAN DIEGO

Adelaide's

7766 Girard Avenue
La Jolla, CA 92037
(619) 454-0146

This is one of those rare examples of a superb shop where many years of business and a large volume haven't jaded creativity or put a crimp in quality. Adelaide's stands behind every product; if you are dissatisfied with an arrangement, it will be picked up and replaced. The shop's many designers can more than adequately cater to both ends of the design spectrum. Just be sure to tell them what you want.

The selection of giftware and specific holiday ideas, whether for Valentine's Day or Christmas, is dazzling. What's particularly noteworthy is the huge inventory of flowers. "The notion of cash-and-carry cut flowers started here thirty years ago. The entire front of our shop opens onto the street like a large open market." You can hardly walk by without being tempted to buy something special, and you will be assured of good value.

Minimum: $30.00 plus delivery
All major credit cards
Also serves: San Diego area—East County, North County and South Bay

SAN FRANCISCO

A Bed of Roses
PAT POTOVSKY AND PAT MILLER

2274 Union Street
San Francisco, CA 94123
(415) 922-5150

A Bed of Roses is an appropriate name for this charming, tiny, well-stocked shop, which also sells a myriad of lovely accessories and clear-glass vases of flowers. The work here is strongly influenced by ikebana, and the arrangements convey an artistic flair. The results are stylized—and spectacular. You can find lots of potted plants, perennials, annuals and vines here, too.

Minimum: $30.00 plus delivery
All major credit cards
Also serves: East Bay area and Marin County

Bloomers
PATRICK POWELL

340 Presidio Avenue
San Francisco, CA 94118
(415) 563-3266

At Bloomers you'll find lush bouquets that border on the Flemish style. In less talented hands the work might appear heavy, but Patrick magically imbues mass with poise. Even his Biedermeier-inspired arrangements of all-white flowers, combining lilacs, anemones, tulips, narcissus and ranunculus have a cool vibrancy. Great examples of his work are the arrangements he did for Alvin Horton's book, *Arranging Cut Flowers* (San Francisco: Ortho Information Services, 1985).

Handsome overscaled shelves are filled with carefully chosen porcelain cachepots, baskets, terra-cotta containers and a wide selection of glass vases in just about every size and shape.

Patrick's discriminating eye extends to his little shop next door, filled with the most exquisite French ribbons, both old and new, as well as Fortuny pincushions, sachets of potpourri, and pillows. You'll also find delightful headbands and a sampling of some of the many decorative accessories that he's found on his travels.

Minimum: $30.00 plus delivery
All major credit cards
Also serves: East Bay area and Marin County

Fiordella
JEAN THOMPSON AND BARBARA BELLOLI

1920 Polk Street
San Francisco, CA 94109
(415) 775-4065

Jean and Barbara have a flair for combining tropicals with English-garden flowers. Their work is so simply elegant, they make it look easy. But I've seen many designers who've tried the same combinations and failed.

Jean and Barbara are not afraid to take risks that challenge the imagination. Their arrangements shock the eye into appreciating and loving a unique way of doing things—similar to what Robert Joffrey did for ballet.

This Italianate shop is painted a wonderful Tuscan orange and sports bleached-wood tables and waxed terra-cotta-colored floors. It is filled with fresh flowers, blooming plants and orchids as well as a bountiful supply of containers, many of which the shopkeepers buy on their annual trip to Italy. It's Italian with a California sensibility.

Minimum: $25.00 plus delivery
All major credit cards
Also serves: East Bay area and Marin County

IXIA
GARY WEISS

2331 Market Street
San Francisco, CA 94114
(415) 431-3134

The key words here are *high style, exotic* and *tropical,* for IXIA deals mainly in the unusual. The selection is drawn from all over the world: tropicals from Hawaii and Central America; proteas, banksias and leucadendrons from Africa, Australia and New Zealand; and dozens of varieties of orchids, orchid plants and bromeliads grown locally or imported from Hawaii and Southeast Asia. In addition to the exotics, IXIA carries a large selection of unusual garden flowers bought from European and local growers. Vines, gnarled roots, weeds, fruits, vegetables, rocks, weathered wood and mosses are some of the less conventional elements used in designs. Even the shop's traditional European-garden arrangements have that distinctive IXIA twist.

Whether the occasion calls for a quiet, graceful look with Japanese simplicity or something bolder and more dramatic, with a colorful, playful feeling, one can always expect the unique style for which IXIA has become well known.

Minimum: $35.00 plus delivery
All major credit cards
Also serves: East Bay area and Marin County

SAN MARINO

Milo Bixby, Inc.
MILO BIXBY

2640 Mission
San Marino, CA 91108
(818) 799-7143

Although Milo has been in business some thirty years, his work is always fresh and up-to-date. He specializes in English country bouquets. He's another genius who can find beauty in something as lowly as a peanut hull and include a bunch of them in a delightfully surprising presentation with just the right flowers and foliage.

Minimum: $35.00 plus delivery
All major credit cards
Also serves: Altadena, Arcadia, Glendale, Pasadena and San Gabriel

SANTA BARBARA

Gazebo Flowers
SCOTT HOGUE

P.O. Box 5475
Montecito, CA 93150
(805) 969-1343

After owning a very successful restaurant, Scott decided to "retire" to the flower business. Now he's busier than ever, simply because he loves flowers, and it shows. Many dedicated gardeners grow solely for him, and the result is diversity: "I can get lots of fresh lavender and things you just can't get in the market." He also gets five-foot delphiniums and even taller foxgloves. It's no surprise when he says, "I love doing size. My work is very natural, as though I went into a field and picked the flowers myself." Don't let that deceive you: It takes a great deal of talent to achieve simplicity.

For a romantic gift for two or one large enough for a family, try his sumptuous picnic baskets. Since Scott's a man of several talents, he knows his food and his flowers.

Minimum: $35.00 plus delivery
Credit cards: MasterCard and VISA
Also serves: Carpinteria, Goleta and Summerland

SANTA CRUZ

Antonelli's Floral Design
PETER BABBIT, MANAGER

2545 Capitola Road
Santa Cruz, CA 95062
(408) 475-8828

It's ironic that here, in the heart of America's floriculture industry, many of the local people are not acquainted with the vast variety of flowers available at Antonelli's. Peter's access to just about any type of flower is unparalleled in this country. You should take advantage of his enthusiastic willingness to go directly to the growers for just about anything you may want, whether it's tulips in July or floribunda roses in December.

Peter's studio-style shop, located in the center of America's largest begonia nursery, is filled with locally grown flowers, Holland imports and lots of tropicals, which he uses in styles ranging from loose and airy casual creations to strong-line contemporary manipulations. European hand-tied bouquets can be had on request. Peter's inventory of herbs and blooming plants is also inspiring. Be specific about what you want; if you're not sure, a good rule is to ask for whatever is in season and abundantly available.

Minimum: $25.00 plus delivery
Credit cards: MasterCard and VISA
Also serves: Aptos, Capitola, Soquel and Watsonville

SANTA ROSA

Ireko
JIM RASCO AND MIKE WEBB

509 Seventh Street
Santa Rosa, CA 95401
(707) 579-3700

J im Rasco studied bonsai with the American master of the art form, John Naka, and his shop is well stocked with exotic bonsai that he has "brought on" himself. While they are pros at true ikebana, Jim and his partner, Mike Webb, have developed an expertise using cut flowers that results in a free-form look. Wherever on the design spectrum they are working, "the flowers speak for themselves. We work to their benefit and our clients' desires."

The shop is filled with an eclectic but well-chosen variety of interior accessories that complement the flowers. From Japanese and French antique containers to proprietary metal, glass and ceramic objects d'art, it's all part of providing a complete interior design service. "We don't try to have something for everybody here, but we do have something new for everybody to see. It's fun for us and for our clients. . . . That's what's most important!"

Minimum: $35.00 plus delivery
All major credit cards
Also serves: Healdsburg, Petaluma, Rohnert Park, Sebastopol and Sonoma

SONOMA

Taylor's of Sonoma
BILL TAYLOR

147 East Spain Street
Sonoma, CA 95476
(707) 938-1000

A number of florists in this handbook do English-garden-style arrangements. What makes each one special and different from the other is the particular approach and the materials he or she uses. Bill Taylor's unique approach to his decidedly English look is the bold use of native materials such as California bay, broom or milkweed, combined with flowers and herbs grown locally, as well as Holland imports. His mixed bouquets are casual but special.

We all should be thankful for florists like Bill, those who go the extra mile, combining innovation with talent.

Minimum: $25.00 plus delivery
All major credit cards
Also serves: Agua Caliente, Boyes Hot Springs, El Verano, Eldridge, Fetters Hot Springs, Glen Ellen, Schellville and Vineburg

TAHOE CITY

Wanda's Flower Shop
WANDA BAMBERY

P.O. Box 5337
Tahoe City, CA 95730
(916) 581-2180

Wanda started her business as a plant-leasing and maintenance company. Soon after, her clients, having grown accustomed to her reputation for quality and integrity with foliage plants, asked if she would start working with flowers as well. Her business expanded along commercial lines, with weekly standing orders for restaurants and model homes in the area. Now she has the best selection of fresh flowers in town in addition to her foliage and blooming plants.

Wanda's predominant style is a high contemporary one, displaying a strong Oriental influence and often incorporating props such as bamboo or painted leaves or pods. She is capable of creating loose, country bouquets, which she is often called upon to do for weddings.

A perfect gift order from Wanda's is a wrap bouquet of selected flowers. Be specific about what you want; the usual bouquet is a mix of gladiolus, iris, Peruvian lilies, larkspur, stock and tulips. Wanda carries a nice variety of tropicals also. Loose bouquets go out wrapped in cellophane and tied with satin ribbon, raffia or "paper" ribbon—your choice. For arrangements, she has dozens of baskets, glass bowls—especially black ones—and some specialty unglazed ceramics. Again, specify your preferences.

Minimum: $25.00 plus delivery
Credit to be arranged
Also serves: In California: Truckee; in Nevada: Incline Village

53

TIBURON

Main Street Floragarden
PATRICK AND MARCIA MAFFEI

116 Main Street
Tiburon, CA 94920
(415) 435-9260

There is an easy feeling about this shop; it can be overloaded with orders, and you would never know it. Everybody is calm and personable, which is a number of notches above being professional. The same goes for the arrangements. They are natural, and nothing is forced. It takes a great deal of talent to achieve this sort of unassuming simplicity, which is appropriate anywhere.

Minimum: $25.00 plus delivery
All major credit cards
Also serves: Corte Madera, Fairfax, Ignacio, Larkspur, Mill Valley, San Francisco, San Rafael, Sausalito and Terra Linda

WEST HOLLYWOOD

Zen, A Floral Design Studio
ROSEWOOD HOTELS, INC.

501 North Robertson
West Hollywood, CA 90048
(213) 274-3495

This is a satellite of the Zen store headquartered in Dallas. They also have a small boutique in the Bel Air Hotel, just up the hill from this store. For a detailed description of their work, please refer to the entry for Zen in Dallas.

Minimum: $40.00 plus delivery
All major credit cards

WOODSIDE

In Any Event
Rick Davis and Anne Dickey Schoebel

2934 Woodside Road
Woodside, CA 94062
(415) 851-3520

While known for their colorful, country-style planted baskets, Rick and Anne also do lovely English arrangements. The decision of which one to order should be left up to them, as it's a matter of what's the freshest and best in their shop that day. That's integrity!

This store is brimming with gifts and plant accessories; some cute and fun, others sophisticated and serious.

Minimum: $35.00 plus delivery
Credit cards: MasterCard and VISA
Also serves: Atherton, Hillsborough, Menlo Park, Mountain View, Palo Alto, Portola Valley, Redwood City and Sunnyvale

COLORADO

ASPEN

The Flower Shop
Tony Dumire

601 East Hopkins
Aspen, CO 81611
(303) 925-5430

Everyone has a place where they like to spend time—somewhere that feels like home and pleases the senses. The Flower Shop is just such a place. High in the Rockies, surrounded by unequaled beauty, The Flower Shop caters to the customer's personality—whether a movie star, a business mogul or just plain folk.

The shop is always filled with wonderful things: grapevine garlands and baskets, dried peonies, delphiniums, roses and hydrangeas; Balos and Blenko vases to complement any style of arrangement; buffalo and deer skulls adorned with dried flowers and made into one-of-a-kind wall hangings; and, of course, the finest mix of fresh flowers available anywhere in the world.

For ten years The Flower Shop has filled the floral needs of people who know and want the best. From the smallest arrangement to the grandest production, it is known for its professionalism and respect for a client's particular taste. People have been heard to say that it's "indescribably delicious—better than the finest chocolate." A friend of mine who is a nationally known art collector recently said, "The Flower Shop is a national find."

Minimum: $35.00 plus delivery
All major credit cards
Also serves: Snowmass Village

BOULDER

Country Squires
DAVID SQUIRES

722 Main Street
Louisville, CO 80027
(303) 666-4906

Davidcombines imported flowers that are handsome and important, such as lilies, calla lilies, tulips and roses, with garden perennials like columbine and delphiniums. Then he adds herbs and wildflowers for a spirited though traditional expression. For a more flamboyant look, he'll use imported

Holland flowers with tropicals, such as heliconias, Oriental pineapple or spathiphyllum. While he may have a clear idea of what kind of arrangement he's going to make, the flowers are never forced into a preconceived position. The natural movement of each flower is respected; nothing is contrived or manipulated. There's life and rhythm in his presentations.

Arrangements are done almost exclusively in clear glass. "Flowers simply last longer in water, and besides, the look of clear glass or Lucite lends itself best to our neoclassic-inspired designs," says David. The decor of his shop, reflecting this orientation, is a beautiful flannel gray with impressive white crown molding.

Country Squires carries Aromatic potpourri and is expanding its line of gift containers. David comes up with creative solutions to holiday gift giving, so be sure to ask about them.

Minimum: $20.00 plus delivery
All major credit cards
Also serves: Denver and Longmont

Gentry's
TERRY GENTRY

21 South Tejon
Colorado Springs, CO 80903
(719) 632-0707

Terry's daily work is imbued with a French country feeling. He combines a wealth of garden flowers in a casual way, almost exclusively in clear glass containers, unless you request one of his wonderful twig baskets or an in-house moss and twig creation. "I am inspired by anything romantic. I love soft, free-flowing arrangements; however, I am also known to do what I refer to as pseudo ikebana for a more exotic, contemporary look," he says.

His flowers come from all over the world, but he takes great advantage of local flora like chokeberry branches, scrub oak, grasses from the plains and cultivated wildflowers. And he always carries tropicals.

Seasonal herb gardens, potted perennials and flowering bulbs, as well as an extensive choice of blooming plants—and orchids whenever he can get them—complete a well-rounded selection for us to choose from.

Minimum: $35.00 plus delivery
All major credit cards

DENVER

Bouquets
ALBERT J. FEEGER

2908 East Sixth Avenue
Denver, CO 80206
(303) 333-5500

What keeps this charming shop's distinctly natural-looking arrangements from being quaint is Albert's dedication to just the right look. He ensures a level of sophistication by growing his own greens, all the twirly bits that the English take for granted but American florists often overlook. Albert and his associates are very capable of high-style, contemporary work as well. A stop at Bouquets is just the right antidote for a busy day. The shop is immaculate, carries an abundance of very fresh flowers and, best of all, smells like a spring garden.

To serve a town like Denver, a florist must have broad skills. Whichever one of Albert's you choose to take advantage of, the end product will be close to perfect.

Minimum: $20.00 plus delivery
All major credit cards
Also serves: Aurora, Castle Pines, Cherry Hills Village, Englewood, Glendale, Greenwood Village, Lakewood, Littleton, Lowry AFB and Wheat Ridge

VAIL

Bird of Paradise Florist
BETTY VANOSDOL

P.O. Box 9
Minturn, CO 81645
(303) 827-5958

W hen you go to Vail, you're a little bit far from the genesis of most things other than snow. In a situation like this, you go to the shop that does the most volume. If all else fails, at least you know your flowers are fresh, not icebox-stale. Betty arranges flowers for most of the lodges and hotels in Vail, so her inventory turns over with some predictability. Whatever your plans are here, keep them simple.

Minimum: $10.00 plus delivery
All major credit cards

CONNECTICUT

GREENWICH

Jardiniere
JANET WALES

41 Williams Street
Greenwich, CT 06830
(203) 661-3154

I t's rare to meet someone in floristry with awe-inspiring talent who can keep as great a sense of humility as Janet has, especially considering her accomplishments in the flower world. She's as terrific with people as she is with flora, and it's no wonder that anyone with whom she does business adores her.

With the highest standards, she creates one masterpiece after another in the European style, stressing the beauty of the flowers themselves. She's well trained and well disciplined yet imbues her works with a romantic flair. Her arrangements comprise a controlled abundance of imported Holland flowers, including tulips, freesias, lilies and roses. She rarely uses tropicals.

Janet says she becomes "excited by the beauty of a single flower. After all," she asks, "why always put flowers in arrangements. A single stem of Casablanca lilies or a hybrid rose is dramatic in itself. Sometimes it's a waste to mass them all up together."

Minimum: $35.00 plus delivery
Credit to be arranged

Nijole's Flowers
NIJOLE VALAITIS

3 Field Road
Cos Cob, CT 06807
(203) 661-1045

Fifteen years ago, after the demands of motherhood had lessened, Nijole opened her shop. She already had developed a very loyal clientele while free-lancing out of her basement. "I've always done a sort of English look," she says. "As you can imagine, loose and airy wasn't in style fifteen years ago, so my arrangements were not as popular then." Thanks to the courageous vision of people like Nijole, we can have flowers as we do today.

Although her talents enable her to create almost anything, there are two styles that predominate in Nijole's work. She moves from very loose and airy arrangements to Japanese creations, particularly in the style of the Sōgetsu School. "Whatever I do, I am known for my unusual color combinations: I am not afraid to combine oranges and reds or pinks and oranges. And the focus is always on the flowers, not the idea."

Nijole's shop is filled with antique containers of all sorts that she has collected during her travels. A number of decorators find it a great source for vases. She also carries topiaries, orchid plants, French and Dutch flowers, and bromeliads, as well as exotic tropicals from Hawaii.

Minimum: $25.00 plus delivery
All major credit cards

HARTFORD

The Flower Boutique
JEAN E. GLAZIER

15 South Main Street
West Hartford, CT 06107
(203) 233-2603

Refreshing English-garden arrangements combining Dutch imports and seasonal garden flowers give Jean her exceptional reputation. Yet she's very capable of contemporary work as well. Although she rarely carries tropicals, she enjoys the occasional order for high-style arrangements.

When asked to describe a work that was particularly spectacular, she enthusiastically responded, "Everything I do is my favorite." Her work is essentially seasonal. She has a rare, high regard for hybrid Dutch chrysanthemums and an equally strong disregard for liatris. "It's a pretty color, but too unnatural-looking," she explains, "as if it were plugged in, electrified."

Holiday ideas abound here. For Valentine's Day last year, she made fresh heather hearts with roses floating up through the center, the hearts set in low baskets with two white doves.

Minimum: $25.00 plus delivery
All major credit cards
Also serves: Bloomfield and Farmington

NEW HAVEN

Jasmine
DAVID GEORGE AND DAVID GILLMAN

1 Elm Street
New Haven, CT 06510
(203) 785-1430

Integrity and style are evident throughout this shop. In order to maintain their high standards, it's not unusual for the Davids and their associates to turn down orders when they find themselves overwhelmed. This is especially true during holidays, so be sure to get your orders in early.

Local and imported flowers are all hand-selected and combined with a deft touch to create loose, lovely bouquets that go out in glass containers or baskets. There is also a tempting selection of Italian glass, terra-cotta and antique containers to choose from. The Davids maintain a wonderful array of blooming perennial plants—delphiniums, foxglove, bleeding heart, or lilies—that can be used for gifts. This is certainly a step beyond the standard choice of mums or azaleas. Topiaries and orchids are on hand as well. Enchanting table arrangements range from massed bouquets in thirty-eight-inch glass vases to flowers artfully strewn right on top of the table.

In keeping with their philosophy of carrying one-of-a-kind items, the Davids maintain an exclusive inventory of antiques, primarily American: a country pine drop-leaf harvest table; Hepplewhite dining chairs; French tapestry pillows. You'll even find an antique Chinese wedding kimono—just one good thing after another.

Minimum: $40.00 plus delivery
All major credit cards
Also serves: Branford, East Haven, Hamden, North Haven, Orange,
West Haven and Woodbridge

NEW PRESTON

The Cottage Garden
SARAH STOCK

Main Street
P.O. Box 2297
New Preston, CT 06777
(203) 868-2886

Resting on the banks of the East
Aspetuck River in historic New Preston, The Cottage Garden is
housed in a restored general store. Sarah spends her days making
fresh and dried arrangements, using some of the flowers gathered
from her old-fashioned flower and herb garden.

Her work is a welcome relief from the same old Holland
flowers you see over and over, because she's able to take great
advantage of her riverside garden. Imagine the arrangements you
see in Flemish paintings, with flowers like phlox, bleeding heart,
penstemon and honeysuckle, and you'll have an idea of the kind
of work Sarah can do.

In the winter she resorts to flowers carefully chosen at
market, which she combines with flora from her greenhouse, such
as flowering strawberry, forced branches and bulbs, scented geraniums and a host of herbs.

Minimum: $25.00 plus delivery
Credit cards: MasterCard and VISA
Also serves: Litchfield

The Drummer Trading Company
CHRIS ZAIMA

Route 45
New Preston, CT 06777
(203) 868-9914

Chris is a significant talent whose romantic floral masterpieces have highlighted many interiors in *Architectural Digest* and *Metropolitan Home*. For years he was a free-lancer, but he recently joined forces with a group of aesthetically minded friends to head up the floral efforts of The Drummer Trading Company.

While Chris can provide the expected services of a florist, you should take advantage of his imaginative drive to create unusual, personalized gifts. For instance, if you're sending a gift to someone who likes ivy, Chris searches out ten or twelve species of the ivy genus, *Hedera,* and artfully juxtaposes them in an antique terra-cotta or English ironstone container. A similar treatment is given to the mint family—many different kinds in a whitewashed wooden crate accompanied by an attractive explanatory card. His gifts are gorgeous, educational and interesting, but most of all they are thoughtful reflections of his customers' needs.

Chris combines classic techniques with his own visceral sensibilities, unleashing a vision that takes advantage of the local seasonally available materials: Vegetable and fruit baskets are filled with locally grown produce, and the basket handle is wrapped with baby tomato vines ripe with pendulous, jadelike fruits, accented with a bouquet of garden-fresh zinnias. Picnic baskets include local wines and your choice of the freshest foods from The Drummer's charcuterie, all graced with a bouquet of herbs. If you want to send cut flowers to somebody and know, for example, that the recipient has a fabulous container in the entrance hall, Chris will go there himself to compose the bouquets. These are just a few examples, given to shake you loose of preconceptions, expand your imagination and provide a glimpse of the possibilities here. My advice is, talk to Chris, find out what he's excited about and give him free rein.

Minimum: $100.00 for cut flowers; $50.00 for planted baskets
24-hour notice required
Credit to be arranged
Also serves: Litchfield, New Milford, Washington and all of Litchfield County

OLD LYME

Old Lyme Jardiniere
DEBORAH OSCAR

P.O. Box 423
Old Lyme, CT 06371
(203) 434-8501

"Special occasions deserve the singular style of this shop." So goes the advertising jingle accurately heralding the style and service at Old Lyme Jardiniere. The arrangements here are loose and airy, and you won't see the hard line often associated with contemporary presentations. Deborah handpicks her flowers at market, carefully selecting specific varieties, such as the pale pink la rêve lily. The same pride goes into selecting foliage; ruscus, boxwood and English ivy.

The shop is abundantly stocked with topiaries, especially reindeer and bears at Christmastime. Partridgeberry wreaths and boxwood Christmas trees lavishly decorated with dried flowers are other holiday creations.

All arrangements are carefully wrapped in tissue and cellophane and tied with French ribbons, each with an oval card printed with the shop's handsome logo.

65

Minimum: $30.00 plus delivery
Credit cards: MasterCard and VISA
Also serves: Essex, Lyme and Old Saybrook

SOUTHPORT

Candace Newton
CANDACE NEWTON

P.O. Box 637
Southport, CT 06490
(203) 254-3487

Candy's free-lance business flourishes in her studio overlooking the Southport harbor. Three phone lines bring in one request after another. "Perhaps it's because I like to create unconventional illusions that are inventive and fun—but most important, flowers and atmospheres must be pretty," says Candy. She mixes Holland flowers with seasonally available local flowers, foliages and herbs. "My arrangements are at home with antique Battenberg lace." Daily gift orders go out in clear glass containers or baskets.

Although Candy is a free-lancer, she offers many alternatives to cut flowers for gifts. She sets lush blooming plants into antique baskets, juxtaposing them in garden fashion, and cuddles them in hump moss or the trunks of unusual topiaries with live mosses, then drapes them with French ribbons. Whatever your choice, Candy's sensitive eye and talented hands deliver extraordinary results.

Minimum: $100.00 plus delivery
3 days' notice required
Credit cards: MasterCard and VISA
Also serves: Darien, Fairfield and New Haven

STAMFORD

Muguet Florists
SIMIN MODJALLAL AND HASHEM KHATIBI

189 Bedford Street
Stamford, CT 06901
(203) 356-8999/358-8944

After working in Paris, Simin launched a successful free-lance career in Connecticut beginning with large hotel accounts. She opened this shop several years ago because she needed a base from which to serve her growing clientele. Her style incorporates a minimum of green foliages. "Instead I fill up an arrangement with flowers—enchantment lilies, dendrobium orchids, champagne roses—flowers that have long-lasting qualities and are fragrant," says Simin. Her elegant arrangements always go out in clear glass unless you request a basket or other container, such as a gold- or platinum-leafed vase or one of the handmade Japanese ceramic pieces she carries. Blooming plants are presented in natural baskets or conventional terra-cotta pots.

From her tiny shop, tucked away on a small side street, her reputation for stylish integrity has spread by word of mouth. What struck me as particularly noteworthy is that the shop is virtually cleared of all flowers by the close on Saturday, to be replenished on Monday, and again on Thursday, by flowers Simin or Hashem handpicks from market.

Minimum: $35.00 plus delivery
All major credit cards
Also serves: All of Fairfield and Westchester counties

NOBU Florist
Alec Armstrong and Nobutaka Shiina

135 Main Street
Stamford, CT 06901
(203) 348-6795

Nobu studied Sōgetsu, a specialized version of ikebana, for many years in Japan, and consequently his shop specializes in what he calls an Americanized version of Japanese arranging: Holland imports and lots of tropicals combined into high-style compositions with a strong focal point. He's also adept at country baskets.

Most flowers are imported, but from time to time "we get lucky," says Mr. Armstrong, "and somebody local brings in orchids, foliages or flowers they have grown. We have a local grower for annuals."

Arrangements go out in glass containers, baskets or "upscale" plastics. They do carry lovely Oriental antiques, but the focus here is on the flowers, either fresh or silk, and not on gift accessories.

Minimum: $30.00 plus delivery
All major credit cards
Also serves: Darien, New Canaan, Norwalk and Wilton

WESTPORT

The Flower Basket
Charles Case

995 Post Road East
Westport, CT 06880
(203) 222-0206

Anything said about Charles can only touch the surface of his talent. His bouquets are luscious and abundant. Everything is sweet and natural, but imbued with an aura of sophistication—an almost impossible combination of moods. Charles's skills are so finely tuned that he can evoke even the subtlest emotions.

He carries his own pottery vases, made in assorted colors, and baskets woven from raspberry canes, honeysuckle vines and native grasses. His own holiday potpourri, a pine and citrus combination, makes a great gift when combined with flowers.

Charles's arrangements appear in several publications, especially books by Martha Stewart.

Minimum: $40.00 plus delivery
All major credit cards
Also serves: Fairfield, Greens Farms, Southport and Weston

DELAWARE

WILMINGTON

Bloomsberry Flowers, Ltd.
Denis L. Chandler

1725 Delaware Avenue
Wilmington, DE 19806
(302) 654-4422

Unless you have access to a large estate garden, the kinds of materials that Denis uses in his very natural, seasonal arrangements are simply not available. I spoke by phone with him late one fall afternoon while he worked in the garden behind his shop. He grows all kinds of wonderful things there—witch hazel, red-stemmed dogwood, blackberry lilies and goldflame honeysuckle—as well as in his well-cultivated wildflower field and perennial beds. He creates woven tapestries of flowers and foliage and, when appropriate, incorporates fruits, nuts, branches and berries into his arrangements. Specially made baskets or glass containers are used for daily gift orders. Stunning potted flowering plants change with the seasons.

This is a dream of a shop, designed as a home library and full of dog-eared reference books and lovely illustrated tomes for information or inspiration; they are available for clients' use as well. Mantles, mirrors and Oriental rugs complete a warm and inviting place to visit. We all can be inspired by a sincerely dedicated person like Denis who deeply loves flowers and knows how to enjoy them.

Minimum: $25.00 plus delivery
Credit cards: MasterCard and VISA
Also serves: In Pennsylvania: Centerville, Chadds Ford, Greenville and Kennett Square; in Delaware: Hockessin, Newark, Rockland and Talleyville

Flowers, Plants & Gardens
HERBERT S. PLANKINTON, JR.

5725 Kennet Pike
Wilmington, DE 19807
(302) 656-2400

For many years Herb Plankinton has been a much sought after floral designer and decorator on the Wilmington and Philadelphia scenes. A growing demand for his dramatic floral statements convinced him to open his own shop in April of 1987. He believes that only when you work and live with flowers on a daily basis can you train your eye and "liberate your imagination."

His shop is located in an eighteenth-century three-story brick building that used to be a general store. Behind the shop is a spacious double gazebo filled with plants and flowers, which opens onto an acre of gardens punctuated with fountains and lined with cobblestone paths. Both the depth of Herb's knowledge and his skill as a designer in the outdoor world of plants and flowers are obvious here.

The shop, painted in jet black and poison green *faux* marble, is filled with decorative accessories, vases in every shape and size and exotic gifts from around the world. An inviting refrigerated garden room complete with French doors and neoclassic-style garden furniture holds masses of cut flowers from local growers and many parts of the globe as well. Customers are invited to roam, picking whichever flowers they want. There's a host of creative ideas to take advantage of here, with just the right amount of splash and dash.

Minimum: $40.00 plus delivery
Credit cards: MasterCard and VISA
Also serves: In Pennsylvania: Centerville, Chadds Ford, Greenville and Kennett Square; in Delaware: Rockland

Wanda Freeman Flowers
WANDA FREEMAN

124 School Road
Wilmington, DE 19803
(302) 656-9734

Ms. Freeman creates country arrangements in the homes of many of her clients on a regular basis, maintaining a personalized slant to her work. "For example," she says, "if somebody is in the hospital, I like to send magazines with the arrangement; ones that I know the recipient will enjoy. I incorporate special things that the person likes in a very natural, gardeny arrangement. My work tends toward the traditional." Flowers are arranged in glass cylinders or vases, hand-blown bottles or baskets, all of which are part of a large and very tasteful selection.

Wanda uses seasonal flowers and branches from local gardens with her imports. Rarely does she carry tropicals. "I like to select my flowers personally from the wholesalers, because, undoubtedly, their idea of pink is different from mine."

Minimum: $30.00 plus delivery
Credit to be arranged

Also serves: In Pennsylvania: Centerville, Chadds Ford, Greenville and Kennett Square; in Delaware: Rockland

DISTRICT OF COLUMBIA

Bluewillow, Ltd.
EDWARD SCHANHOLTZER AND PATRICK DOYLE

1729 20th Street, NW
Washington, DC 20009
(202) 234-9600

Although their shop is very architectural—with an arched half-wall and black and white terrazzo marble floors—Messrs. Schanholzer and Doyle's work is very free, soft and flowing. Mr. Doyle says, "That's one reason we do so much wedding work. It's romantic, not Victorian; lots of stems show. Our arrangements are very light and airy."

Most arrangements are in the classic European style, with a contemporary flair. They carry a wide variety of baskets, terracotta, ceramics and other original containers for their arrangements.

Minimum: $35.00 plus delivery
All major credit cards
Also serves: In Maryland: Bethesda, Chevy Chase, Potomac and Rockville; in Virginia: Alexandria and McLean

David Ladd & Company, Custom Flower Design
DAVID LADD AND TOM RANNICK

1622 Wisconsin Avenue, NW
Washington, DC 20007
(202) 337-0413

This shop is small, charming and understated. David and Tom have the style and ability to create one beautiful arrangement or wonderfully decorate a party for five hundred. If you're unsure of what's in good taste, then defer to David. He knows what's right.

David and Tom describe their mission as "adding the sparkle and elegance to a room without anyone knowing a florist has been there." They use either English-garden flowers or tropicals.

Minimum: $35.00 plus delivery
All major credit cards
Also serves: In Maryland: Bethesda, Chevy Chase, Potomac and Rockville; in Virginia: Alexandria and McLean

Washington Harbor Flowers by Angelo Bonita
ANGELO BONITA

3050 K Street, NW, Suite 145
Washington, DC 20007
(202) 944-4600

This is a big company, and Angelo has big ideas—and I'm sure he'll succeed. Many florists desperately try to be all things to all their clients; it's the rare and talented designer who can master a dozen different looks. Yet Angelo has tackled this problem head-on and solved it in a unique way. Over the years he's developed his business to the point where he can support an international team of thirteen artists who offer any look you want.

The layout of Angelo's new shop mirrors this approach to the business. You enter a large, glitzy carpeted room around which are approximately fifteen design "stations." It is at these stations that his designers practice what he or she is best at, from Oriental design to English romantic arrangements. Angelo truly understands that he cannot be all things to all people; a shop can be, however, if you hire the best from each school of design.

Minimum: $45.00 plus delivery
All major credit cards
Also serves: In Maryland: Bethesda, Chevy Chase, Potomac and Rockville; in Virginia: Alexandria and McLean

FLORIDA

DELRAY BEACH

Jennings Jardiniere
EDIE ("JENNY") AND JOE JENNINGS

806 NE Ninth Avenue
Delray Beach, FL 33483
(407) 272-1661

Jenny modestly describes her favorite arrangements as "gardeny, and loose. . . . Something that looks like the customers could do it themselves." Yet I cannot stress enough the skill that goes into creating this simplicity. The Jennings rely on the Holland market for most of their flowers but of course look to Hawaii for their tropicals. Unless otherwise directed, arrangements are done in clear glass. Jenny has a great selection of handsome grapevine and painted woven baskets appropriate for arrangements or planted presentations. The latter are recommended for their ability to withstand Florida's hot and humid climate, which is so hard on cut flowers.

Jennings' has a greenhouse full of foliage and blooming plants, lots of orchids (varieties that the proprietors pick personally on their visits to Hawaiian suppliers), and bedding plants. They're often called upon to design patio gardens for their customers. "We don't put in two-inch plugs [small, seedling plants]. The plants we install are mature, large and in full bloom, as though they've been growing there for some time. When our clients come to town, they want their homes ready for a party the minute they arrive," says Jenny.

There's an abundance to draw on here for gifts, but you should especially take advantage of Jenny's knowledge of what is best for certain times of year. Having been in the area for almost twenty years, she probably even knows the recipient. For example, she hardly ever recommends loose cut flowers in wrap bouquets. In Florida's climate, they'll hardly make it through their destination's front door. And herbs are a problem because of the red spider mite.

The presentations of potted plants or orchids, unless you request something special, go out in simple terra-cotta pots "with a minimum of frill," says Jenny.

Minimum: $25.00 plus delivery
Credit cards: MasterCard and VISA
Also serves: Boca Raton and Palm Beach

FORT LAUDERDALE

Collica
VICTOR COLLICA

824 East Las Olas Boulevard
Fort Lauderdale, FL 33301
(305) 764-8000

Victor combines masses of flowers, such as French spray roses, sweet peas, anemones and hybrid delphiniums; a variety of wildflowers, such as Queen Anne's lace and lisianthus; and trailing vines that spill over the sides of containers—creating full, romantically Victorian bouquets. His arrangements are soft, almost buttery, and just right. With talent like this, a dislike for certain flowers that are contrary to his style is inevitable.

The shop is always full of imported fresh flowers, blooming plants and select orchids, but Victor carries no giftware other than special holiday creations. A glorious example of these are his Easter eggs rubbed with pigment and decorated with painted Etruscan motifs or given a *faux* finish. Victor and his associates concentrate on their first priority—arranging flowers beautifully.

Minimum: $40.00 plus delivery
All major credit cards
Also serves: Miami to Palm Beach

JACKSONVILLE

Richard's, Inc.
RICHARD STUART

3617 St. John's Avenue
Jacksonville, FL 32210
(904) 387-2525

For thirty years Richard Stuart has striven to be the first with fresh and innovative ideas for flowers and parties. This goal keeps him busy enough to make him wonder whether he might not enjoy the relaxation of being number two instead of number one.

Richard proudly states that although he doesn't specialize in any particular style, whichever style is chosen by a client is carefully designed to meet exacting standards. Whether it's parrots shaped from fresh flowers, hand-tied European bouquets or a ballroom ceiling decorated with papier-mâché angels, Richard claims that you'll always get flowers and decorations presented uniquely.

The gifts and accessories at this shop are as imaginative as the flower ideas. You'll find a wide variety of items, from fruit and vegetable works by Mary Kirk Kelly to Chinese porcelain, Italian terra-cotta and the finest silk flowers.

Minimum: $25.00 plus delivery
All major credit cards
Also serves: Jacksonville Beach, Mandarin and Ponte Vedra Beach

MIAMI

The Brickell Avenue Flowers & Plant Shop
RICK ANDREWS

1013 Southwest First Avenue
Miami, FL 33130
(305) 374-8471

Each arrangement here, whether it's high style or a loose garden bouquet, has a small package of tulle-wrapped raspberry-scented potpourri attached to the gift card. Thoughtful touches like this, and Rick's quality and assortment of flowers, have engendered enough popularity to enable him to open another shop, Bayfront Flowers, in the Intercontinental Hotel. Twice a week flowers are shipped directly from Holland to be combined with his vast assortment of Hawaiian and Southern Hemisphere tropicals. His favorite flowers are lilies, from stargazers and rubrums to Casablancas and enchantment lilies. He gathers as many locally grown hybrid lilies as he can.

Daily arrangements are usually done in clear glass, although Rick inventories fabulous baskets and the requisite contemporary containers. He and his associates are particularly fond of tropical foliages; it's not unusual for an arrangement to incorporate twelve different kinds of exotic leaves and vines. If you order a large arrangement, they like to incorporate an entire orchid plant that can be kept long after the other flowers in the piece have been discarded.

There are many gifts here to choose from: life-size stuffed animals, English and Oriental antiques and everything imaginable for the table. Access to a top-notch gourmet store provides champagnes, caviars, pâtés, wines and fresh-baked breads for gift baskets. Blooming plants are available as well. Be specific about what you want, and it's sure to be presented with elegance and a dash of glitz.

Minimum: $30.00 plus delivery
All major credit cards
Also serves: Hialeah and Kendall

NAPLES

The Flower Gallery
RICHARD DEXTER AND ANTHONY SMITH

707 12th Avenue, S
Naples, FL 33960
(813) 262-5446

The Flower Gallery aspires to an eclectic look: "Flexibility is our forte," says Mr. Dexter. Styles range from traditional ikebana to contemporary high style to romantic Flemish bouquets. What sets this shop apart from many that use a wide spectrum of styles is an antischooled philosophy. According to Mr. Dexter, "The best designers are those whose skills have been developed naturally while their aesthetic sensibilities were being nurtured. So often, a schooled approach dampens the instinctual spirit that is crucial to any kind of good design."

Flowers are shipped in from all over, and spectacular ones at that: six-foot heliconia, white anthurium, and parrot tulips. Daily arrangements go out in glass, custom-made containers or baskets. Their gift line includes Oriental containers, Italian terra-cotta and good-quality crystal. Foremost, their energies are focused on the flowers.

Minimum: $25.00 plus delivery
Credit cards: MasterCard and VISA
Also serves: Marco Islands

PALM BEACH

Rick van Horn
RICK VAN HORN

129 Hammon Avenue
Palm Beach, FL 33480
(305) 832-5338

Talented, attractive, fun—these are just a few of the words used to describe Rick van Horn. People who know him love him, and women who depend on his talents say they derive more pleasure from his flowers than from a dress Arnold Scaasi made for them. He's one of those free-lancers whom we're very lucky to have in this handbook, because an arrangement by Rick is truly a gift—a profusion of flowers in a truly grand style.

Minimum: $50.00 plus delivery
24-hour notice required
Credit to be arranged

SAINT PETERSBURG

Delma's Flower Booth
DELMA BOOTH

2448 Fifth Avenue, N
St. Petersburg, FL 33713
(813) 327-3232

Although the variety of local tastes demands that Delma not limit herself to one style, she does confine herself to tasteful and elegant design. Tropicals, garden flowers and Holland imports are all constants in her inventory, and they are used to create exactly what her customers want, from Oriental designs to country arrangements. She says, "If you tell me the feeling you want, I'll go from there." She's been in business since before I learned to walk, so she undoubtedly knows what people in Saint Petersburg like.

Take advantage of her unusual greens, such as maranta and black mahogany leaves, and all kinds of dracaenas and ferns. She maintains a terrific assortment of orchids and foliage plants as well.

Minimum: $25.00 plus delivery
All major credit cards
Also serves: Pinellas Park, Seminole and all Gulf beaches

SARASOTA

Rainforest
LOUISE CHAPPELL

5108 Ocean Boulevard
Sarasota, FL 34242
(813) 349-3554

Louise previously owned an antique store and has always been involved with interiors. Consequently, she likes to know the context in which her arrangements will be placed. She prefers Victorian combinations of wildflowers and Holland imports, but believes a jug chock-full of white tulips can be equally effective.

Arrangements go out in baskets or cylinders covered in moss or leaves and tied with raffia or handsome ribbons. "Nothing should ever look as though it came from the florist," says Ms. Chappell. She loves antique jewelry and is locally well known for the way she works a piece into an arrangement for a special gift. Her tiny store is full of well-chosen antiques and dried flowers, too.

Minimum: $25.00 plus delivery
All major credit cards
Also serves: Longboat Key, Osprey and Siesta Key

TALLAHASSEE

Jessie's Florist
JESSIE PLAINES

3425 Thomasville Road
Tallahassee, FL 32308
(904) 893-1863

Jessie acknowledges that the fundamental motivation for sending flowers is the desire to express a sentiment. With every order she and her associates strive to fit the flowers to the occasion. "We send romantic bouquets for anniversaries and engagements, distinguished ones for funerals, and contemporary, high-tech designs for the opening of an office," says Jessie. Whatever the occasion, Jessie or one of her designers enjoys hearing exactly what a customer wants—from the choice of flowers to the preferred container.

This is the only store in town that sells Holland flowers, so this is where you'll find the widest selection. It's florists like Jessie, who design with an innovative but considerate instinct, that have taught us to enjoy the new aesthetic that has revolutionized the floral industry.

Minimum: $25.00 plus delivery
All major credit cards

TAMPA

Floral Impression
HARRISON GIDDONS

4203A El Prado Boulevard
Tampa, FL 33629
(813) 837-2027

Hyatt Regency–Westshore
Retail Suite C
Tampa, FL 33607
(813) 837-2027

Harrison Giddons started free-lancing out of her garage five years ago, filling weekly orders for corporate accounts, weddings and parties. Eventually the demand for small gift orders grew so great that a retail shop seemed logical. "It still amazes me," says Harrison, "how few people realize we do a regular, day-to-day floral business. So many people think we just do very expensive things."

Her work has a sophisticated southern look: Native foliages such as magnolia and split-leaf philodendron are used, and each flower in her compositions stands out on its own. Most of the flowers are shipped in from all over the world. "Our climate is so hot and buggy," Harrison explains, "that it's hard to grow the perennials and other garden flowers we like to use."

Arrangements go out in either clear glass containers or baskets. Inexpensive containers are often wrapped in moiré taffeta or hot-glued with moss, when appropriate. The shop always carries orchids, bromeliads and other blooming plants.

Gift items are mostly accessories for table settings, such as candles, votive holders and napkin rings. If you're ordering a holiday present, be sure to ask what inspired gift item is available.

Minimum: $25.00 plus delivery
All major credit cards

VALPARAISO

Stevens and Van Dyke Florist
TAMI AND RICK VAN DYKE AND RICH STEVENS

418 Government Boulevard
Valparaiso, FL 32580
(904) 678-7395

Four years ago Stevens and Van Dyke was just a small-town garden center with a lot of ideas and a reputation for quality. When the proprietors decided to expand their services beyond landscaping, the next logical step was to add a full-service floral department. At that time, however, nobody associated with the nursery had any experience with the business. Interview after interview yielded no results. Then luck and fate took over and dropped Butch Henley on their doorstep.

John D. ("Butch") Henley IV has been in the floral industry ever since he was big enough to carry out the trash. Both his father and grandfather were in the business. Add to that a bachelor of science in botany, a natural gift for public relations and an indomitable enthusiasm for the flower business. Thus Butch has brought an even greater standard of excellence to an already outstanding business.

"We are always looking for what is new and exciting in the floral industry, because if you don't grow, you die. And even though we are located in a small town, our clients are mostly retired people and military personnel who have been all over the world and know quality when they see it. We are rarely asked to do 'roundy moundies' because these people for the most part want designs with an Oriental or European flair."

Minimum: $20.00 plus delivery
Credit cards: MasterCard and VISA
Also serves: Destin, Fort Walton Beach, Mary Esther, Niceville and Shalimar

VERO BEACH

Deb's Flowers For You, Incorporated
DEBBIE SAWYER LIETZ

6120 North A1A
Indian River Shores, FL 32963
(407) 231-6215

No one look typifies the work in this shop, but seasonality is a consistent thread throughout all the work here, whether the materials are imported cut flowers or blooming plants. Styles range from high-style contemporary to traditional to cozy French country bouquets in baskets. This kind of flexibility is often necessary in smaller towns, and consequently you need to express your preferences. Containers range from terracotta pots to baskets, clear glass containers and contemporary ceramics. Debbie, a bird lover, will incorporate miniature wooden or feather birds into arrangements when appropriate, as well as ribbons of all sorts.

Debbie is inspired by holidays to do exciting in-house designs. Last Christmas her creations featured copper-colored or verdigris accessories such as angels, copper-paper ribbon and reindeer. Combining them with bay leaves, eucalyptus or traditional Christmas greens, plus white or red flowers such as tulips and amaryllis, produced a very festive look.

Minimum: $25.00 plus delivery
All major credit cards
Also serves: John's Island

GEORGIA

ATLANTA

The Cottage Garden
RYAN GAINEY AND TOM WOODHAM; DAVID LAVOY, MANAGER

3165 East Shadowlawn Avenue, NE
Atlanta, GA 30305
(404) 233-2050

The atmosphere at The Cottage Garden is warm and robust, but its creations are decidedly romantic. When I was visiting the shop, the designers were making a gift for a newborn baby girl. They rolled a topiary bunny rabbit in dried lavender flowers, made a ponytail of braided ivy and created a lovely little garland headpiece of the tinniest buds. They placed a nosegay in the bunny's front paws and set her skipping through a field of wildflowers—a delight to see.

This kind of imagination goes into everything at The Cottage Garden. It's the kind of shop where you fall in love with flowers.

Minimum: $30.00 plus delivery
All major credit cards
Also serves: Dunwoody, Marietta and Sandy Springs

Michal Evans Designs
MICHAL EVANS AND SCOTT SCHRANK

34 Irby Avenue
Atlanta, GA 30305
(404) 365-0200

Michal describes his work as "contemporary European with a lot of texture and a touch of fantasy." His signature arrangement employs a great number of imported flowers, like tulips, delphiniums and freesias, with a Hawaiian tropical "tucked in" for surprise.

When you enter this shop, you're immediately impressed by the high standard of taste and the forceful discipline to live up to those self-imposed standards. Everything is "right." You won't see a stuffed animal displayed next to an eighteenth-century urn. The look of the shop is contemporary with a strong neoclassic influence. It's a calm oasis in the middle of a town that's grown too fast for its zoning laws.

Special gift items are created for holidays, and local artists are commissioned to make proprietary ceramic and porcelain vases. Hellenic-style urns with unusual finishes—tarnished gilt, *faux* bronze or burnished copper—are among the fine accessories you'll find here.

Minimum: $35.00 plus delivery
All major credit cards
Also serves: Dunwoody, Marietta and Sandy Springs

Marvin Gardens
BEN LaCOUNT AND MARVIN GARDENS

99 West Paces Ferry Road
Atlanta, GA 30305
(404) 231-1988

Here you'll find robust blends of Hawaiian tropicals and Holland imports—lilies, orchids and spathiphyllum—that add up to big and important arrangements with more than a dash of glitz.

On holidays Ben and Marvin go for the spirit. Here's a sampling from their last Valentine's Day "fantasy menu":

- "Little Red Riding Hood's Basket"—a glossy lacquered red basket full of cupid-red and white tulips or mixed with colorful flowers—perfect for all those big bad wolves in your life!

- "Bear Hugs and Kisses"—a potpourri bear with candy kisses and flowers sitting on a lacquered bamboo tray.

- A traditional Cupid's kissing ball topiary of Marvin Gardens's signature potpourri, Exotica, combined with moss and sweetheart roses intertwined with glistening metallic cords.

A selection of these tempting ideas, and others, are printed up and mailed on handsome stationery to customers. They're having fun at Marvin Gardens, and we can too!

Minimum: $30.00 plus delivery
All major credit cards
Also serves: Dunwoody, Marietta and Sandy Springs

The Potted Plant Ltd.
RYAN GAINEY AND TOM WOODHAM

3165 East Shadowlawn Avenue, NE
Atlanta, GA 30305
(404) 233-7800

This shop preceded Ryan and Tom's other shop, The Cottage Garden. But instead of cut flowers, this shop deals only with growing things. The same love of all things romantic that characterizes what you'll find at The Cottage Garden is applied here to potted-plant compositions.

The designers do lovely baskets or pots using combinations of three or four different plants—azaleas, maidenhair fern and stargazer lilies bedded in mood moss and accented with French ribbons, for example. When their plant arrangements are combined with their fabulous antique containers—urns, wire baskets or porcelains—the results are stunning, one-of-a-kind gifts.

Minimum: $30.00 plus delivery
All major credit cards
Also serves: Dunwoody, Marietta and Sandy Springs

AUGUSTA

Templeton's Flowers and Gifts
BILL TEMPLETON

1125 Green Street
Augusta, GA 30902
(404) 724-4841

In Bill Templeton's shop, an old Spanish-style house with arched windows and Oriental rugs scattered throughout, you'll find a fire going during the winter and rooms filled with birdhouses of finches and canaries. This is a place that people of all ages love to visit. Fresh flowers are everywhere, and a sun porch off the side of the house is a jungle of potted plants and orchids.

Bill creates loose European bouquets that he says "don't look like they came from the florist. We use lots of glass cylinder vases or grapevine baskets, raffia and twigs, or curly willow, and blossoms of all sorts." Although he imports most of his flowers, during the summer he has garden roses and summer annuals grown specially for the shop. "You can hardly beat a vase full of twenty or thirty full-blown garden roses for a sensational gift."

Bill is always coming up with creative gifts for Mother's Day, Christmas and other holidays. Last year for Mother's Day he had chintz-covered baskets made up specially for the shop, and he filled them with plants or cut flowers: the baskets became so popular that he has to keep an assortment on hand all through the year.

Minimum: $30.00 plus delivery
All major credit cards
Also serves: Evans and Martinez

COLUMBUS

Michael Jarvis
DRAKE AND MICHAEL JARVIS

3760 Woodruff Road
Columbus, GA 31904
(404) 324-6529

"Our emphasis is on style. That's our number one priority," states Michael Jarvis. "It's the only thing that separates us from the grocery stores." The Jarvises' work falls into two categories—traditional English-garden designs suitable for the antebellum houses in the area, and very high-style contemporary arrangements. As Michael puts it: "Our goal is to create an arrangement that fits into the environment it is intended for. Our clientele is very sophisticated, and it is not unusual for someone to order a mass of yellow lilies or tuberoses loosely arranged in a clear glass cylinder."

Their flowers are shipped directly from growers three times a week, so you can count on freshness and variety. Local growers supply them with seasonal annuals, but they don't have a supply of locally grown perennials. (Michael's floral talents are so well regarded, though, that it's not unusual for his customers to bring in their own garden flowers for him to arrange.) The Jarvises head for the woods and fields to gather materials like wild mushrooms, lacy gray lichens, and branches, which are incorporated into compositions when suitable.

Michael carries the entire line of Crabtree & Evelyn products, including food items, potpourri and soaps, to send along with flowers. The usual blooming plants are available, such as kalanchoe, geraniums, azaleas and primroses.

Minimum: $25.00 plus delivery
All major credit cards
Also serves: In Georgia: Fort Benning; in Alabama: Phenix City

MACON

Lawrence Mayer Florist
LAWRENCE AND JONATHAN MAYER

587 Cherry Street
Macon, GA 31201
(912) 743-0221

Macon is one of the few southern towns that survived the destruction of the Civil War. All those wonderful antebellum houses and the unique flavor of the town guide Lawrence Mayer's work toward natural English bouquets with a slight Flemish cast. Roses, delphinium, lilies, freesia, lilac and ranunculus blend together to create a full romantic image. He can achieve the same look using tropicals. Occasionally ikebana slips into Mr. Mayer's repertoire, but his way with ikebana is also graceful and soft, not composed of contrived hard lines.

The shop is filled with blooming plants and gift items such as antique Chinese porcelains, crystal, unusual baskets and lots of clear glass vases. Don't ask for orchids; growing them is such a big hobby in Macon that they don't make popular gifts.

Minimum: $30.00 plus delivery
All major credit cards

ROSSVILLE

Ensigns
BILL AND CONNELLY ENSIGN

1300 South Crest Road
Rossville, GA 30741
(404) 866-0155

Bill describes his work as having a natural look. The arrangements I've seen are positively vibrant: baskets full of wild flowers, weeds and Holland imports. The concern for detail is obvious in everything he does. Lots of his flowers, perennials like astilbe, yarrow, larkspur, and scabiosa, are grown locally.

Bill does wonderful traditional arrangements with important flowers like lilies, tulips and amaryllis. He has a real talent for planted compositions and arranges great-looking combinations of foliage and flowering plants in terra-cotta containers or baskets for indoors or outside.

Minimum: $25.00 plus delivery
All major credit cards
Also serves: In Tennessee: Chattanooga and Lookout Mountain

THOMASVILLE

Singletary's Flowers & Gifts
JIMMY, RAMSEY AND PEGGY SINGLETARY

512 South Broad
Thomasville, GA 31792
(912) 226-5880

Located in the heart of the South's grand plantations, Singletary's creates one graceful arrangement after another. They excel at loose, gardeny arrangements filled with local materials. One flower you should take advantage of here is the garden-grown rose. From April through October local growers keep this shop stocked with masses of them—both old-fashioned varieties and new hybrids. When these are out of season, a wonderful bouquet can be made by mixing native greenery such as smilax, cedar and holly with Holland imports like tulips, freesia or lilies. The combined inventory of local and imported material makes for a huge selection of flowers and foliages to choose from. Arrangements go out in glass containers, baskets or terra-cotta pots.

Singletary's "European Nature Baskets" are a local favorite. Grapevine baskets are filled with blooming and foliage plants such as gardenias, azaleas and hibiscus, and the arrangement is punctuated with mosses and native mushrooms and often accented with branches. These grand arrangements are perfect for the foyer of a plantation house, or "even to take apart and spread the plants throughout the house," says Jimmy. Singletary's is an enthusiastic, creative shop where the customers and the flowers come first.

Minimum: $25.00 plus delivery
All major credit cards
Also serves: In Georgia: Barwick, Boston, Coolidge, Meigs, Ochlocknee, Pavo and Quitman; in Florida: Monticello

HAWAII

HONOLULU

City Florist

1133 South King Street
Honolulu, HI 96814
(808) 536-7002

The owners of City Florist say their biggest competition is the supermarkets. After being in business for fifty-one years, they know that their future depends on their continued ability to interpret their clients' needs and create lovely arrangements. Many of their flowers are brought in from San Francisco, but of course fabulous tropicals and beautiful tea roses are grown nearby. There's no demand for bulb plants here, so don't ask for potted tulips or paper-whites, but seasonal blooming plants and orchids are kept in stock. Design styles here range from European bouquets to ikebana-influenced compositions. Arrangements go out in glass vases, wicker baskets, or contemporary containers.

Minimum: $30.00 plus delivery
All major credit cards

MAUI

Floral Designs
BARBARA SCHENK

181 Pauhana Road
Makawao, Maui, HI 96768
(808) 572-6262

Barbara's studio is nestled upcountry amid acres of cultivated orchids. As a free-lancer, she divides her time between demanding corporate and hotel accounts, weddings and individual gift orders. Her styles range from the traditional to glitzy contemporary work, depending on the occasion; but for gifts being sent to vacationers from the mainland she encourages the client to go tropical, whether you send one of their unique leis or a florabundant vase of local tropical flowers. "After all," Barbara explains, "the local tropicals such as heliconias, anthuriums, orchids and other native plants are reasonably priced and exude the full flavor of Hawaii."

Barbara gleans lots of local materials from the roadsides and hills, such as unusual thistles, bamboos, weathered palm bark and banyan tree roots, and combines them with locally grown tropical flowers, lilies and roses. Garden flowers are shipped in from California and Holland. She keeps a large inventory of containers in a variety of materials, including ceramics, clear glass, baskets and heavy-gauge plastics. Attractive bamboo containers are made in-house as well. She's known for her unusual combinations of flowers as well as her artistic flexibility. Give her the essential parameters—budget, type of container and style of bouquet—then leave the details to her magical imagination.

Minimum: $25.00 plus delivery
Credit to be arranged
Also serves: All areas of Maui except the back side of the island, Hana

IDAHO

BOISE

Boise Floral
RON SCHOLTEN

822 West Idaho
Boise, ID 83702
(208) 345-6011

Though the guiding concerns of this full-service florist shop are flexibility and efficiency, it made its mark in Boise with its bold, high-style contemporary designs. "People appreciate the visual impact of these strong-line minimalist arrangements," says Mr. Scholten. A diverse inventory of fresh flowers here enables Ron to do just about anything, so be specific about what style you want, the flowers you prefer and the type of container, from clear glass vases or baskets to heavy-gauge plastic pots in assorted decorator colors. A variety of blooming and foliage plants is also available.

Minimum: $25.00 plus delivery
All major credit cards

SUN VALLEY

Sun Valley Florist
SUE BRIDGEMAN AND KATHY ESTES

P.O. Box 1055
Sun Valley, ID 83353
(208) 622-4587

You can get just about everything to do with flowers here: planted patio pots, custom Christmas decorations, foliage and blooming plants, orchids, dried flowers and masses of cut flowers, shipped in from all over the world, as well as locally grown seasonal treats like sweet peas, spirea, calendula and asters.

Daily arrangements go out in clear glass; however, a great selection of unusual baskets and terra-cotta containers are kept in stock.

Arrangements are usually loose, airy and natural, and the designers take great advantage of all things local. One of Sue's favorite arrangements is a combination of rose hips in season, native grasses and garden flowers . . . wild, romantic, drop-dead splash!

Minimum: $25.00 plus delivery
All major credit cards
Also serves: Ketchum, Hailey, Bellevue, Stanley and Carey

ILLINOIS

BARRINGTON

Fresh Flower Market
IRIS KLUG

213 West Main Street
Barrington, IL 60010
(312) 381-7800

Located on the first floor of a quaint cottage, Fresh Flower Market is cleverly divided into two spaces. The first is the gift shop and conference section, and through that you enter the tiny flower shop, which is actually a large cooler in disguise. In this sparkling white, sun-drenched room, forty or more buckets of flowers arranged on the floor or placed on the ledges of the bay window envelop you in a hypnotic fragrance and a kaleidoscope of colors and shapes. It's the kind of shop where you hope everybody is too busy to help you—you just want to sit and soak it in.

Arrangements are stylishly country, like the baskets overflowing with Holland imports and locally grown perennials. All of Iris's work is charming and exciting!

Minimum: $25.00 plus delivery (next-day delivery is available to Chicago and suburbs)
Credit cards: MasterCard and VISA

CHICAGO

City Garden
GAY H. ROBERTS

312 South Dearborn
Chicago, IL 60604
(312) 427-6600

Cy Garden is Chicago's fresh new source for floral designs. Located in the landmark Monadnock Building, its six-hundred-square-foot mirror-wrapped flower gallery has custom-bleached maple woodwork and Carrara marble floors and display surfaces. This look gives the shop a cool, professional ambience in which lovely arrangements of all sorts are created, from classic European bouquets to florabundant tropicals.

Ms. Roberts's corporate background with Tiffany & Co. instills a professionalism and dedication to quality in this fine store, as does her well-trained eye for talent and beauty. She and her team are setting standards that the floral industry ought to emulate.

Minimum: $40.00 plus delivery
All major credit cards
Also serves: All of Chicago and surrounding suburbs

Flowers By Clody
DOROTHY RUNGE AND HENRY COLLINSON

3200 North Broadway
Chicago, IL 60657
(312) 327-1842

In Henry's truly original work you'll see two styles of design: two vertically parallel focal points softened by freesias or various lilies, alstroemeria and heather; and a strong *S* line form similarly softened.

The shop is filled with ostrich eggs, Murano vessels and terra-cotta containers. Henry works up his own, wildly architectural baskets. He knots long, wide sheaths of grasses and raffia through the upper edges, giving them an aboriginal feel. These baskets become objects in themselves, rather than just containers for flowers.

Minimum: $30.00 plus delivery
All major credit cards
Also serves: All of Chicago and surrounding suburbs

GLENCOE

The Flower Shop
ROBERT LIVERMORE

693 Vernon
Glencoe, IL 60022
(312) 835-5390

Stepping into Robert's shop is like walking into a well-landscaped garden. Although the space is small, flowering plants and tall topiaries are well laid out on varying levels in drifts of color punctuated by well-chosen gifts. An exemplary arrangement on a pedestal draws your eye to the back of the shop.

Arrangements produced on a day-to-day basis are sophisticated, voluminous and romantic.

Minimum: $30.00 plus delivery
Credit to be arranged
Also serves: Downtown Loop, Highland Park, Lake Forest, Northbrook, Winnetka and near west suburbs

MOLINE

Rock Valley Florists
KATHY MISTIC

3009 18th Avenue
Rock Island, IL 61201
(309) 794-0312
(800) 798-0312

The modus operandi at Rock Valley Florists is to be accommodating to customers. "If there's something you want, and it is available, we'll do our best to get it for you," says Kathy. Their day-to-day inventory includes carnations, mums, daisies and select Holland flowers, as well as the expected seasonal blooming plants such as cyclamen, kalanchoe or chrysanthemums. In addition, Kathy has sources for wonderful annuals like zinnias and sunflowers during the summer, as well as orchid plants, perennial plants and tropicals. Just give her notice, be specific about your desired presentation, and you can depend on her to do a good job. If you're in a hurry, a glass bubble full of white carnations, daisies or white roses tied with raffia is a good idea, or perhaps a basket planted with a mix of blooming and foliage plants.

Minimum: $20.00 plus delivery
All major credit cards
Also serves: In Illinois: Rockport; in Iowa: Davenport and Bettendorf

WILMETTE

The Crest of Fine Flowers
MEDARD C. LANGE

417 Fourth Street
Wilmette, IL 60091
(312) 256-3900

Here is another of those immensely talented florists who have been influencing tastes and trends in this business for many years. As a testimony to his unyielding dedication to what's stylish and tasteful, Mr. Lange is the florist to a third generation of clients. His predominant style is abundant bouquets of seasonal flowers and greens, very natural and soft. Upon request he will create a dramatic, highly styled arrangement.

The shop is filled with excellent gifts—the best of Mottahedeh, Val St. Lambert and Herend. There is also a selection of Louis XVI–style antiques. A wonderful collection of urns, both old and new and of all shapes and materials, can be found here as well.

Minimum: $25.00 plus delivery
Credit to be arranged
Also serves: Chicago, Deerfield, Evanston, Highland Park, Kenilworth, Lake Forest, Northbrook and Northfield

WINNETKA

Mary Lee McClain
MARY LEE MCCLAIN

458 Maple Street
Winnetka, IL 60093
(312) 441-7283

Elegant and imaginative, Mary Lee's talents achieve opulence through simplicity. A natural use of space and flowers allows grace and ease to penetrate every arrangement. Mary Lee's southern upbringing is evident in the warmth and sincerity of her work. She takes the time to feel the inherent rhythms of the imported flowers and native branches she works with, so nothing is studied or harried and everything is perfect. It's as if her arrangements speak that southern sensibility of "Let me do something special for you"—a warm touch of hospitality.

Minimum: $35.00 plus delivery
Credit to be arranged
Also serves: Evanston, Glencoe, Kenilworth, Northfield and Wilmette

INDIANA

BLOOMINGTON

Ellis Floral Company
Jay Ellis

2500 East Third Street
Bloomington, IN 47401
(812) 332-7201

Jay is the third generation to carry on the Ellis tradition in flowers. The business has expanded significantly over the years and now serves as a full-service florist and party planner. The Ellises do everything for a party except the food: They will plan the flowers; supply the tent, chairs and table cloths; rent costumes; choose the lighting and, sometimes, even the music. Their floral styles are equally expansive, including everything "from the 'roundy moundies' to high-style contemporary," says Jay. Flowers come from all over the world, but not from local growers.

A nice gift from the Ellis Floral Company would be a basket of planted perennials. Jay used to be in the nursery business, and he still has contacts with local greenhouse growers for herbs and perennials for planting. For cuts, a bouquet of lilies or tulips will do. Keep your plans simple, and be specific about what you want.

Minimum: $30.00 plus delivery
All major credit cards
Also serves: Clear Creek, Ellettsville, Smithville, Stanford and Unionville

INDIANAPOLIS

Edna Woodard
EDNA WOODARD

4745 Kessler Boulevard, North Drive
Indianapolis, IN 46208
(317) 291-7918

Mrs. Woodard's garden-flower arrangements are unique in Indianapolis, and consequently her free-lance flair is in great demand for weddings, charity galas and private parties. Her basket bouquets, with a garden look of seasonally available flowers, such as garden roses, Queen Anne's lace, delphiniums, campanula and thyme, are natural, easy and friendly with that perfect dash of sophistication. Her friend and mentor is Sheila Macqueen, so it's understandable that her work is English-inspired.

Mrs. Woodard stocks a collection of containers as well as the baskets she uses in most of her work.

Minimum: $100.00
24-hour notice required
Best at market
Credit to be arranged

Wells Flower & Gift House
Diane Wells

2160 West 86th Street
Indianapolis, IN 46260
(317) 872-4267

Seven telephone operators direct incoming calls to the fifteen rooms of giftware and flowers that make up this shop. Regarding flowers, store manager Donna Writt says the operative design concept is "Less is more." That translates to a look utilizing a few choice blooms in a strong-line contemporary display. Being a full-service florist shop, Wells can create just about any design you want, but you must be very specific. As suggested by the size and scope of the store, there's a lot more going on besides flowers: children's clothes, china, wicker furniture, paper products and gourmet candies, to mention but a few.

The choice of containers is as vast as the selection of giftware. A nice gift would be a bunch of rubrum lilies combined with some gourmet foods and wines from the adjoining shop, or perhaps three dozen white roses in a clear glass bubble, tied with ribbon or raffia. Blooming plants are available, but nothing out of the ordinary. A holding greenhouse is full of foliage plants if you want to go that route.

Minimum: $20.00 plus delivery
All major credit cards
Also serves: Brownsburg, Carmel, Noblesville, Westfield and Zionsville

SOUTH BEND

Wygant's Floral Company
MIKE BAUER AND MARY GREEN

327 Lincoln Way, W
South Bend, IN 46601
(219) 232-3354

The first priority here is a strong concern for value buttressed by a wide variety of flowers, all bought at market. With this emphasis on value, the designers here will arrange greenhouse-grown roses in bud, or send out flowering plants either foil wrapped or dropped in a hat and decorated with pussy willow arched to form a "handle" with a bow on top. Whatever your taste, Wygant's strives to live up to its reputation for quality and care. Keep your plans simple and be specific: say, a hundred white carnations massed in a glass bowl, or four terra-cotta pots of Reiger begonias.

Minimum: $20.00 plus delivery
Credit cards: MasterCard and VISA
Also serves: Granger, Lakeville, Mishawaka, New Carlisle and Osceola

IOWA

CEDAR RAPIDS

The Flower Shop at Cedar Park

4200 First Avenue, NE
Cedar Rapids, IA 52402
(319) 393-8004

There is variety and versatility in this shop; and because it's doing volume work and is lucky to have dedicated talent, this is the place to go for flowers in Cedar Rapids. There is a warm energy here, and a sincere willingness to please. Just be specific about what you do and don't want.

Minimum: $30.00 plus delivery
Credit cards: MasterCard and VISA
Also serves: Hiawatha and Marion

DES MOINES

Carriage Florist
MARLEY SMITH AND AUBREY DUNBAR

2711 Grand Avenue
Des Moines, IA 50312
(515) 282-9109

"If you give us a description of the house to which the gift is going, we'll take off from there," says Mr. Dunbar. Indeed, he and Marley Smith can do arrangements appropriate for deco settings, black and white contemporary, English country and more. "It's often funny," says Aubrey. "If one of us is doing a particular style arrangement, somebody in the shop inevitably says, 'I know who that's going to!' "

You can frequently see their work in *Victoria Magazine*. Cranberry wreaths, with each and every cranberry attached with a black boutonniere pin, are stunning. Marley and Aubrey also do a glitzy Hershey's Kiss wreath tied off with silver punch ribbon. And a local favorite as a gift for the hospital is their "Candy Cactus"— many pieces of one kind of candy glued onto a form that gives the whole thing the shape of a standard topiary.

Foliage and blooming plants always go out in baskets. They have orchids whenever they can get them. As yet there hasn't been a big demand for topiaries.

Minimum: $25.00 plus delivery
All major credit cards

KANSAS

TOPEKA

Porterfield's
DAVID PORTERFIELD, AIFD

3101 Southwest Huntoon Street
Topeka, KS 66604
(913) 354-1707

The styles here flow freely from natural gardeny bouquets to stylized, contemporary manipulations that stop short of using painted or dyed materials. Whatever the style you choose, you can be sure of this shop's professionalism. Flowers are shipped in from all over the world, including a wide range of tropicals, while seasonal garden flowers and wildflowers, such as larkspur, peonies or lady's-mantle, are gathered from local suppliers. Vegetables, fruits, wild mushrooms and various seed-pods are often incorporated into arrangements when appropriate. Orchids and blooming plants are available seasonally.

David and his associates design straightforward and affordable gifts for holidays. For example, one Christmas a white-washed basket was filled with ivy, holly and miniature poinsettias punctuated with dramatic twigs and mosses. For Mother's Day, a terra-cotta pot wrapped with voile ribbons held a standard topiary of tightly arranged foliages and roses.

The Porterfields are very involved in the industry. David's wife, Frances, is the publisher of an informative trade magazine, *Florists' Review*. They are up-to-date not only on design trends but also on technology.

Minimum: $20.00 plus delivery
All major credit cards

KENTUCKY

ASHLAND

Dee's Flowers
Roger Vannater

2809 Louisa Street
Catlettsburg, KY 41129
(606) 739-4148

Loose, open styling and an obvious concern with matching the style to the personality of the recipient are typical of Roger's work. An ability to design in all styles—Oriental, Edwardian, Dutch, Flemish, new wave—reflects his multischooled training. If you want a natural arrangement of garden flowers or a florabundant bouquet of tropicals instead, just emphasize your preference. After all, Roger's first priority is to create a mood that fits the client's wishes as well as the occasion. In order to achieve that goal, he asks a lot of questions when an order is placed. Having lived in this area his whole life, he may know the recipient, and may be familiar with his or her home, colors or preferences.

Roger lives on a ten-acre farm, which supports all kinds of native foliage, flowers, reeds and grasses. He also cultivates bulbs, perennials and flowering shrubs and trees. Be sure to take advantage of his willingness to grow and supply special things for his shop.

Minimum: $25.00 plus delivery
All major credit cards
Also serves: In West Virginia: Huntington; in Ohio: Ironton

LEXINGTON

Chase Clark
CHASE CLARK

3544 Creekwood Drive, #12
Lexington, KY 40502
(606) 269-0794

A free-lancer, Chase combines imported flowers with locally grown garden flowers and interesting materials he collects along roadsides and in the woods. His arrangements portray an understated elegance. "If you live with flowers in your house every day, as my clients do," says Chase, "you don't want the arrangements to look as though the house is being staged for a state dinner or something. The flowers need to be natural and unaffected, not grandiose and pompous." Clearly, Chase understands the subtleties of providing the appropriate flowers for his clients.

On a daily basis gift arrangements are done in willow or

grapevine baskets or in baskets that Chase hand-paints. He also uses glass cylinders and pedestal vases. Nothing here is trendy or studied, just simply lovely.

Minimum: $35.00 plus delivery
24-hour notice required
Best at market
Credit to be arranged
Also serves: Frankfort

A Tisket, A Tasket
SARAH DAVIS AND BARBARA CLIFTON

1550 Tates Creek
Lexington, KY 40502
(606) 269-4727

"We do special things for special people. All of our work is unique and personal, and we always design with a sense of the specific occasion in mind, so that the arrangement is appropriate." This is the standard that Barbara and Sarah set for themselves when they started free-lancing three years ago. They are booked up for a year in advance, an obvious reflection of their talents.

Their day-to-day work takes on an English country look. Weeds and wildflowers from the roadsides and fields, flowers from local gardens and Holland imports are combined in baskets or glass bowls. These women are full of great ideas. For Halloween they use corn husks for containers; small poinsettia plants are unpotted and the root balls wrapped with silver painted doilies to serve as Christmas-tree decorations that last a month. "We're discovering new things all the time." The examples are as endless as their efforts.

Minimum: $35.00 plus delivery
24-hour notice required
Credit card: MasterCard

LOUISVILLE

Margaret Kulp
MARGARET KULP

3702 Fairway Lane
Louisville, KY 40207
(502) 895-8067

Large vases containing masses of flowers from the garden combined with imports are the key to Margaret's style. For the past five years she's traveled to England annually to study with Sheila Macqueen and Ann Ord—a floral extravaganza. It's our luxury to bask in her talents.

Margaret is a free-lancer and consequently has to put restrictions on the types of things she'll do. She doesn't make hospital deliveries or do traditional funeral work, for example.

Minimum: $35.00 plus delivery
24-hour notice required
Best at market
Credit to be arranged

LOUISIANA

MONROE

Les Petits Fleurs
DAVID JONES

1105 Forsythe
Monroe, LA 71201
(318) 323-7400

Local people associate the name Donna Price with this shop because her tasteful talents built its

110

reputation. But recently, after she had a baby, she sold Les Petits Fleurs to David, but she still works here regularly, and Donna and David's standards and style grace this shop.

"We strive to deliver the best quality flowers and create arrangements that are definitely styled, but not overworked," states Donna. Her arrangements look like slices of a well-thought-out, well-kept cottage garden. Daily work is done in terra-cotta vases, clear glass containers or baskets. All flowers, primarily Holland imports, are bought from wholesalers. Seasonal blooming plants, such as potted tulips and narcissus, daisies, begonias, geraniums and hydrangeas, are also available. The focus here is on the flowers, so all giftware is horticulturally related; but it's always changing, so just ask what's new.

Minimum: $25.00 plus delivery
All major credit cards

NEW ORLEANS

Flowers Unlimited, by Jesse
JESSE DE LOS REYES

1124 Gravier Street
New Orleans, LA 70112
(504) 524-6567

J esse combines seasonal annuals and blooming branches and bushes locally cultivated for cutting with flowers imported from all over the world. The design skills of his shop span the floral spectrum, from high style to ikebana to country bouquets; he is mostly doing English-garden bouquets and tropicals these days, however, almost exclusively in simple glass containers. That's good for the customer, because flowers last a lot longer in clear water than in oasis. That Jesse succeeds with this method indicates the extent of his talent, since it's harder to design in glass bubbles and cylinders than in oasis, because of the lack of mechanical support.

Jesse's work was seen by anyone who caught Nina's wedding on the daytime soap opera "All My Children."

Minimum: $35.00 plus delivery
Credit cards: MasterCard and VISA

The French Quarter Florist
BOB LeBEAU

223 Dauphine Street
New Orleans, LA 70112
(504) 523-5476/out of state: (800) 992-2909

Seven years ago Bob LeBeau bought this shop and refreshed it with his commitment to quality and to the integrity of design. His underlying goal is to have the freshest flowers in town: "If a flower is just slightly bruised, we don't use it, even if it has just arrived from Holland." At one time he had two shops but found himself spread too thin to be able to keep an eye on quality at both, so he closed the second one.

The talents of Bob and his associates span the spectrum of design styles, from exotic to European to parallel to vegetative. "But frankly," reflects Bob, "we really don't do a whole lot of any of these. Mostly we do just straightforward pretty stuff. Country bouquets, romantic bouquets, that sort of thing."

Minimum: $25.00 plus delivery
All major credit cards

SHREVEPORT

Jack Farmer Florist & Antiques
JACK FARMER

6018 Line Avenue
Shreveport, LA 71106
(318) 869-3297

Naturally sophisticated bouquets are the hallmark of Jack's style. Seasonally available pink roses, rubrum lilies, lavender or white anemones, pink and white gerbera daisies, tulips and lilac comprise the typical palette here. All flowers are handpicked at market twice a week. Jack uses your choice of a clear glass container or a basket to hold your arrangement.

Seasonal blooming plants and orchids are available. "We usually put our plants in stained or color-washed baskets with coordinating paper ribbon that reflects the color of the blossoms instead of contrasting them. It's a dressy look, and certainly not country," explains Jack.

The shop is filled with English antiques, from books to boxes to furniture of either mahogany or burled walnut. Oriental porcelains sparkle throughout the shop. You can't go wrong with the handsome accessories and pretty flowers you'll find here.

Minimum: $35.00 plus delivery
All major credit cards
Also serves: Bossier City

Prentis Brown
PRENTIS BROWN

P.O. Box 4362
Shreveport, LA 71134
(318) 424-3229

Being a world traveler with a national name in floral design, Prentis has the eye and the experience to do very special flowers. His inspiration often comes directly from nature. For example, after spending late summer in the Minnesota countryside, he returned to Shreveport for a wedding he was engaged to do. His flower choices echoed Minnesota's fall colors that so impressed him: pastel salmons, pinks and celadons characteristic of a Midwest fall. Sometimes he will combine garden flowers with selected imports and comb the countryside for branches and grasses that enhance the natural beauty of his arrangements.

After owning a shop for seventeen years, Prentis now freelances and is often called upon to travel on assignment, so you may not always get him. When you do, his splendid talents are certainly worth it.

Minimum: $100.00 plus delivery
2 days' notice required
Credit to be arranged

MAINE

BANGOR

Lougee & Fredericks

546 Hammond Street
Bangor, ME 04401
(207) 947-7102

Versatility is the cornerstone of this sixty-year-old store, and good old-fashioned value the guiding principle. Most flowers are shipped in, however a limited selection of seasonal garden flowers is available during the summer. The store is well stocked with blooming plants, from orchids to birds-of-paradise to chrysanthemums. A selection of premade arrangements, primarily strong-line contemporary ones, is kept on hand in the cooler. "Seven out of ten of our daily requests are for this type of high-style arrangement," explains Bill Sheehan, manager. If you want something simple, I recommend a mass of lilies or white roses or gerbera daisies in a clear glass bubble bowl tied with ribbon and raffia.

Minimum: $20.00 plus delivery
All major credit cards
Also serves: Brewer, Hampden, Orono and Veazie

BAR HARBOR

Fragrant Gardens
ALDA STICH

R.R. 1, Box 2079
Montville
Freedom, ME 04941
(207) 342-5796

Immediately after graduating from the University of Pennsylvania School of Landscape Architecture, Alda moved to her farm in Maine. From the day she began planting her gardens eighteen years ago, she has striven for the perfect balance between ecology and aesthetics. Today, Fragrant Gardens is the culmination of those efforts, a mecca for plants, birds and butterflies.

The carefully planted grounds, laced with lawn paths, are sensational. On display are thousands of flowers, some collected during remote mountain expeditions, some exchanged through international plant societies, and some the product of patient cross-fertilization. You can imagine the unusual flowers and foliages that make up her English-style bouquets, reflecting a true wildflower naturalism. Daily orders are created in your choice of a clear glass vase, basket or large concrete stoneware container.

In order of bloom, her specialties include many varieties of narcissus, primula, pansies, azaleas, columbine, violas, peonies, poppies, roses, bee balm, Queen Anne's lace, lilies, delphinium, campanulas, heather, eryngium, and asters, all available according to season and demand. During the winter months she hand-selects flowers from the Boston markets.

From May through September her gardens are open to the public.

Minimum: $30.00 plus delivery
May–September: 24-hour notice required

October–April: 1 week's notice required
Credit to be arranged
Also serves: Augusta, Bangor, Belfast, Camden and Rockport

PORTLAND

Dodge, The Florist
KEITH DODGE

67 Brentwood Street
Portland, ME 04103
(207) 775-3166

Keith is the third generation to carry on the Dodge family involvement in the floral business, which started in 1920. Although the range of flowers has changed along with the rest of the industry, many traditions are still maintained here. Door-to-door wholesalers deliver the flowers from Boston. Keith relies heavily on these wholesalers instead of ordering directly from Holland, Hawaii or California. Nor does he buy flowers grown in local gardens. His selection is predictable and fresh: tulips, freesias, lilies, carnations, chrysanthemums, hothouse roses, assorted blooming and foliage plants and, occasionally, orchids.

The choice of vases is straightforward but includes very little plastic. A good choice is a simple wrap bouquet or as many of one kind of flower as is in stock: twenty-four fresh rubrum lilies or masses of white carnations in a simple glass bubble bowl.

Minimum: $25.00 plus delivery
All major credit cards
Also serves: Cape Elizabeth, Cumberland Center, Falmouth, Prouts Neck, Scarborough, Westbrook and Yarmouth

D.S. Lillet Fancy Flowers
DANA LILLET

468 Fore Street
Portland, ME 04101
(207) 772-3881

Dana describes her style as an "unstructured, wispy look that incorporates lots of grasses and branches. My favorite flowers are lilies." The shop's black and white tiled floor is dramatically accented with architectural pedestals and columns displaying cylinders of blossoms and branches, grasses and unusual foliages. Dana imports flowers, but also takes advantage of seasonally grown annuals, perennials and herbs. Almost all arrangements are done in clear glass, but a selection of ceramics and baskets is available. If you order loose flowers, they are prearranged and tied with raffia, ready to be recut and placed into your own container. Loose bouquets are presented in a yellow and black box, with polka dot tissue of the same colors and tied with black ribbons. Since Dana places her energies on cut flowers, the only blooming plants available are seasonal bulbs and orchids.

Minimum: $35.00 plus delivery
All major credit cards
Also serves: Falmouth, Freeport, Kennebunkport, Ogunquit and Yarmouth

MARYLAND

ANNAPOLIS

Wildflowers
LAURA VAN GEFFEN AND LISA SHERWOOD

29 Southgate Avenue
Annapolis, MD 21401
Laura: (301) 267-7381/Lisa: (301) 269-1907

Laura and Lisa started out as gardeners, and their passion for flowers grew into a business of arranging them for parties. From four acres of well-cultivated perennial beds they collect the fancy, which they mass with weeds in the Dutch tradition: Lilies, full-blown garden roses and freesias are mixed with blackberry sprigs, crab apples, and grasses. "When you love gardens as much as we do, there is always something special to pick," says Ms. Van Geffen. And they take advantage of imported flowers as well.

Although the choice is not strictly seasonal, the palette often is. From spring's soft pastels to summer's vibrant primary colors to autumn's yellows, reds and oranges, you'll always be delighted to send or receive a masterpiece from Wildflowers. Daily gift orders are delivered in baskets.

Laura and Lisa are free-lancers who collaborate on large parties and weddings; otherwise, they work separately. If you don't get through to one of them, try the other. You can't go wrong.

Minimum: $35.00 plus delivery
48-hour notice required
Credit to be arranged

BALTIMORE

Larkspur
CAROL WESTERLUND

4612 Harford Creamery Road
White Hall, MD 21161
(301) 557-7716

Carol lives way out in the country, and you can imagine all the goodies she can grow to add to her stock of imported flowers. She likes doing things "larger than life." One of her favorite gifts, her "Deep Woods Design," is a centerpiece set in a very low basket. For it she gathers real moss from the woods and mounds it so that two or three short candles can be sunk in flush with the moss. The candlelight glimmers up through lichens, dogtooth violets, white star-of-Bethlehem and tall, tall, tall native grasses with a few jacks-in-the-pulpit here or a Solomon's seal there. Carol says, "The whole thing looks mysterious, but inviting, just like the forest."

Minimum: $45.00 plus delivery
Credit to be arranged
Also serves: Bel Air, Brooklandville, Butler, Cockeysville, Hunt Valley, Lutherville, Timonium and Towson

Secret Garden
ELIZABETH NUTTLE

P.O. Box 586
Brooklandville, MD 21022
(301) 821-1945

Liz is a free-lancer who does not only day-to-day orders, but lots of parties and weddings as well. She also designs perennial borders for many of the local homes. Her horticultural depth shines through her work with cut flowers; her mass arrangements display a sensitivity to both the colors and textures of flowers and foliages. Liz's creative perspective is notably focused on what the arrangement will look like over time: She's concerned with the aesthetic performance of each flower, how a leaf unfolds, how a bud opens up. Fragrance is also an important dimension of her work.

An arrangement from Liz has a natural, gardeny feel to it—controlled and not messy. Her color choices reflect the seasons. For example, during the summer, when the temperature in this area is often around one hundred degrees, she prefers to send bouquets of whites and cool blues: Queen Anne's lace, white roses, blue clematis and both colors of campanulas. Feel free to express your specific desires, or leave it up to Liz. She carefully considers each occasion so that the flowers fit the situation. You can be sure any arrangement will be appropriate and beautiful.

Minimum: $45.00 plus delivery
24-hour notice required
Best at market
Credit to be arranged
Also serves: Butler, Cockeysville, Lutherville, Pikesville, Reisterstown, Timonium and Towson

BROOKEVILLE

Hollywalk Flowers
ANNE BROOKS

211 Brinkwood Road
Brookeville, MD 20833
(301) 774-4983

Anne's arrangements are literally "from the garden." She began her career as a horticulturist with a perennial nursery and evolved into a florist. She grows almost everything she uses but religiously orders freesias, roses, alstroemerias and some lilies. After the growing season she imports most flowers, which she adds to the mosses and twigs she collects from her property.

Although her arrangements are relaxed, their abundant variety keeps them from being simple. "I grow at least eight different campanulas, and I use them all the time," she says, naming artemisia, ornamental grasses and lobelia. The list is as extensive as that of any high-quality perennial operation. Anne also grows many bushes and trees and dries her own flowers.

Minimum: $30.00 plus delivery
24-hour notice required
Credit to be arranged
Also serves: All Maryland suburbs of Washington, D.C., including Bethesda, Chevy Chase and Silver Spring

EASTON

Murdoch Gardens
THE MURDOCH FAMILY

4 North Washington Street
Easton, MD 21601
(301) 822-2778

The Murdoch family has growing operations almost all over the world and also owns a number of businesses associated with flowers. Theirs is a vast operation and yet they maintain very high standards. And this is reflected in their little shop in downtown Easton, where they do lovely work.

Old-fashioned arrangements are put together with imported flowers and those from the garden. "Although we import, we get flowers directly from our growers . . . whether in Bogotá or Holland or Florida. We know everything is fresh, because we've grown it ourselves or we know when it's been shipped," says Mrs. Murdoch.

121

If you're sure of your quality, then a dash of talent goes a long, long way.

Minimum: $20.00 plus delivery
All major credit cards
Also serves: Cambridge, Centerville, Denton, Federalsburg, Oxford, Preston, Saint Michaels, Stevensville and Tilghman

MASSACHUSETTS

BOSTON

Blooming Affairs
BOB SHARRETT AND BOB FELDMAN

79 Park Plaza
Boston, MA 02116
(617) 451-9992

Messrs. Feldman and Sharrett moved to Boston from New York City four and a half years ago, and they took the town by storm. For the last three years they have been the only area florists to win the *Boston Magazine* award for excellence. Their talents cover a broad range, from the grand English arrangements you'd see at Buckingham Palace to the avant-garde. But typically their work is of the latter style, including a great deal of vegetative material in new wave designs. Says Mr. Feldman, "Creativity, along with the most unusual flowers, foliage and plant material flown in fresh from all over the world, makes Blooming Affairs unique."

A box of long-stem roses (thirty-six to forty-eight inches— that's really long!) come enveloped in white tulle with a silver-foil-wrapped chocolate rose on top. Very chic.

Minimum: $40.00 plus delivery
All major credit cards
Also serves: Surrounding suburbs

Tommy Custom Floral Design, Inc.
TOM ROGERS

Le Meridien Hotel
250 Franklin Street
Boston, MA 02110
(617) 426-3925

In 1986, after many years of free-lancing and with numerous corporate accounts in his back pocket, Tommy Rogers opened a retail shop. He still keeps a studio on Thayer Street for large party work and his commercial accounts.

He says his goal is to "create arrangements that get people to stop and stare." And he has succeeded.

His work is so perfect, it's hypnotic—very stylish and tasteful. He achieves a pleasing blend of the traditional and the modern.

Minimum: $35.00 plus delivery
All major credit cards
Also serves: Surrounding suburbs

Victorian Bouquet
SUSAN BATES

53 Charles Street
Boston, MA 02114
(617) 367-6648

Nine years ago, when Susan opened her shop, she didn't expect to be as busy as she is today. But having seen her work, I can understand why she is so successful. The very pretty country-style bouquets she creates in baskets have wide appeal: They are cozy and natural. She has another shop where she arranges and sells dried and silk flowers, but her forte is with the real thing.

Minimum: $25.00 plus delivery
All major credit cards
Also serves: Surrounding suburbs

MARTHA'S VINEYARD

Donaroma's Nursery
MICHAEL AND JANICE DONAROMA

P.O. Box 2189
Edgartown, MA 02539
(508) 627-8366/-8595

Although the Donaroma's main business is landscaping with perennials and other plants for the garden, their talent in creating attractive perennial presentations has led them to start a floral-gift business. After all, what better present to send somebody at a summer home than a basket of blooming lilies or delphiniums that later can be planted in the garden?

Now Donaroma's offers many of the services that florists do, including cut flowers and many different and unusual greenhouse plants, topiaries, bay, broom, leptospermum, orchids, peach hibiscus, various and unusual ferns, bougainvillea and abutilon—to name just a few of the choices. Donaromas' is an attractive and enjoyable nursery to visit, and the staff is exceptionally knowledgeable and friendly.

Minimum: $20.00 plus delivery
All major credit cards
Also serves: All of Martha's Vineyard

NANTUCKET

Flowers at the Boarding House
MICHAEL MOLINAR

12 Federal Street
Nantucket, MA 02554
(617) 228-6007

Down a small island lane in the historic district sits this charming shop in what used to be a carriage house. All sorts of baskets and dried flowers casually hang from exposed ceiling beams. The variety of fresh flowers is breathtaking, from Hawaiian tropicals to Dutch imports to locally grown annuals and perennials.

The arrangements are natural, loose and airy and go out in baskets, clear glass containers or terra-cotta pots. There is a good selection of blooming and foliage plants as well. Topiaries, wreaths and other decorative accessories are constructed from the shop's own dried flowers.

Minimum: $35.00 plus delivery
Credit cards: MasterCard and VISA

NEW BEDFORD

Friendly Flowers
ROBERT CHARON

2301 Purchase Street
New Bedford, MA 02746
(617) 997-4528

Robert's guiding concerns are his devotion to quality and good old-fashioned value. With this in mind he fills the store with affordable flowers such as seasonally available orange and yellow lilies, carnations, chrysanthemums, blue bachelor's buttons, liatris, feverfew, or alstroemeria. Occasionally he has blooming plants—geraniums, hibiscus, cyclamen—but he recommends his bouquets. He likes to know exactly what you want so that he can compose his loose, natural arrangements accordingly.

Hardly anything is available locally, so all of his flowers come from market. "Sometimes we get lucky and I can get armloads of zinnias or even a clutch of sweet peas." If you order a blooming plant, request a basket or simple terra-cotta pot. However, if you want unusual herb topiaries or exquisite orchids, Robert is fortunate to have the famous Allen Haskell greenhouses just up the street.

Minimum: $25.00 plus delivery
All major credit cards
Also serves: Acushnet, Dartmouth, Fairhaven and Freetown

SPRINGFIELD

Burrows Florist
WILLIAM BURROWS

708 Bliss Road
Longmeadow, MA 01106
(413) 567-6181

There are two predominant styles at Burrows: open, airy arrangements that display the flowers' stems through clear glass containers, a sophisticated English style; and vibrant posies in baskets, full of textures and colors, recalling an afternoon picnic in the country. Assorted blooming plants are available to send out singly or grouped in planted baskets or Italian terra-cotta pots. Other than seasonal annuals, all flowers are purchased at market.

The shop is stocked with antiques applicable to flowers:

cachepots, jardinieres, and ironstone. Loose bouquets are wrapped with clear cellophane and tied with your choice of satin ribbon or raffia.

Minimum: $30.00 plus delivery
Credit cards: MasterCard and VISA
Also serves: In Massachusetts: Agawam, Chicopee, Feeding Hills, Hampden, Holyoke, Ludlow and Wilbraham; in Connecticut: Enfield, Somers and Suffield

STOW

One Main Street Studio
C. ANTHONY TODESCO

At The Common
Junctions 117 and 62
Stow, MA 01775
(617) 897-5720

Tony Todesco's talents cover a broad spectrum in the flower world. He is both a designer and a lecturer as well as a nationally accredited flower show judge. His range of styles is just as diverse, from high-tech contemporary work to lovely, natural mixed garden bouquets. He imports many flowers from all over the world, but he's fortunate to have access to seasonal garden perennials, annuals and herbs, such as hostas, rhododendrons, roses, astilbe, sunflowers, zinnias and oregano. This local availability makes such a difference, both in price and in aesthetic depth. Unless you choose one of Tony's antique containers, daily arrangements are done in glass vases, baskets or contemporary ceramics.

Blooming plants, potted herbs, perennials and orchids are available according to season. A thoughtful and exciting gift from this shop is the do-it-yourself arrangement: a big basket overflowing with zinnias and incorporating a selection of shears, gloves, handsome stones, a swath of raffia and a sheet of hump moss. This makes a unique and attractive gift for the person who loves flowers.

Minimum: $25.00 plus delivery
All major credit cards
Also serves: Acton, Bolton, Concord, Harvard, Hudson, Marlborough and Maynard

WILLIAMSBURG

Flower Hill Farm
CAROL DUKE

Hemenway Road
Williamsburg, MA 01096
(413) 268-7481

Carol Duke's unique but convincing style is the result of an artistic talent that's been nurtured by passion and conviction. Through love and hard work she has focused her fine-arts background on flowers to huge success.

After clearing acres of brambles and hedgerow, her gardens are now a proud display of four hundred varieties of perennials, annuals, bulbs and herbs. "Only after hours on my hands and knees, observing a flower through its development, do I really know I understand it and can feel its expression," reflects Carol. It's easy to see how mood dictates her floral selection.

Carol brings all that down-to-earth experience and knowledge to every flower arrangement she creates. Like her gardens, her arrangements show depth and variety, but despite the number of different materials in any one piece, the effect is soothing, not frenetic. Rivers of color are carried through an arrangement by different kinds of flowers, the various species combining in sensual, undulating waves, one next to the other. People have associated her floral work with Monet's paintings, and once you see it you'll understand why.

Minimum: $45.00 plus delivery
May–September: 24-hour notice required
October–April: 3 days' notice required
Credit to be arranged
Also serves: Amherst, Northampton and Springfield

WILLIAMSTOWN

Mt. Williams Nursery
JIM AND KATE ANNICHIARCO

1090 State Road
North Adams, MA 02147
(413) 663-8665

Eight greenhouses of cut flowers form the backbone of this wholesale and retail nursery. "What we don't grow, we import," says Kate. They grow roses, Easter lilies, poinsettias and bulb stock such as tulips, freesia, and paper-whites. To these they add their Dutch and California flowers in cheerful, pretty arrangements reminiscent of a Renoir painting.

"Our arrangements tend to be seasonal. In spring I enjoy combining monkshood, peonies, delphinium, roses or just any in-season garden flowers I can," Kate says. Her daily arrangements go out in glass vases or baskets. She likes to fill bold grapevine baskets with blooming and foliage plants. For summer, combinations of geraniums and maidenhair fern are especially popular.

Minimum: $25.00 plus delivery
Credit cards: MasterCard and VISA
Also serves: In Massachusetts: Adams and Clarksburg; in Vermont: Pownal **and** Stamford

MICHIGAN

GROSSE POINTE

Entertainment Designs
SUSIE V. LAMBRECHT

411 Country Club Lane
Grosse Pointe, MI 48236
(313) 884-4224

Like all great florists who are serious about the business, Susie has gone through many stylistic phases. Although she's capable of designing in any genre, her favorite today is romantic with a decidedly English flair. "When people see my work, they recognize the high quality of the flowers, whether imported or locally grown perennials, meadow or garden flowers," she says. "When I go cross-country skiing, I take advantage of the time to rummage through the woods for inspirational materials, such as lichens, mosses, fungi and branches. Although I love monochromatic schemes, I'm not afraid to use lots of color." From the looks of things, she knows what she's doing.

Susie is more than willing to combine wines and cheeses with flowers for picnics or bon voyage gifts. She says, "I put together all kinds of things, and it doesn't always have to be flowers." She'll also use plants, trees, garden statuary or topiaries. And to add to her talents, Susie has great skill in horticulture. She was once asked to transform a local garden into the styles of one in southern France. She did her homework and imported all kinds of plants indigenous to that region. That's talent!

Minimum: $25.00 plus delivery
Credit to be arranged
Also serves: Bloomfield Hills, Detroit and Troy

HARBOR SPRINGS

Pontius Flower Shop
SANDY HUNTER

592 East Main Street
Harbor Springs, MI 49740
(616) 526-6661

From May through Christmas, Sandy's shop displays fresh garden-grown wildflowers, perennials, annuals and herbs, as well as ones that are imported. Her arrangements are cozy and natural, combining lots of soft colors and textures. The individual faces of the flowers are casually accentuated; nothing is contrived. Clumps of white candytuft peek out from under strawberry foliage, pink geraniums and light blue pansies. Her containers are most often baskets—from rough-hewn branch boxes to natural birchbark ones—or moss-covered containers. The ceiling and walls of Sandy's shop are covered with flowers drying upside down for her dried arrangements, which she calls her "Faded Glory." She extends her talents to silks as well.

Dramatic planted baskets, which Sandy particularly enjoys creating, include up to ten different kinds of blooming plants. Flowers of the same color are grouped to keep the diversity of material from seeming messy or frenetic, while the variety of flower shapes and foliages adds texture, keeping the baskets vivid. Sandy has a lot of tasteful talent, so don't shackle her creativity with too many parameters.

She also prints an attractive brochure of her Christmas decorations and gifts designed and created in-house.

Minimum: $35.00 plus delivery
Credit cards: MasterCard and VISA
Closed: January through April

MINNESOTA

LITTLE FALLS

The Flower Dell
JUDY AND DAVID GLAZE

123 East Broadway
Little Falls, MN 56345
(612) 632-8588

Two hours away from Minneapolis, in Charles Lindbergh's hometown, lies an oasis of talent. Judy and David's work can be sophisticated and restrained or abundantly country.

Although they depend on wholesalers in Minneapolis for their tropicals and Holland flowers, it's their reliance on local gardeners, farmers and collectors that serves as the catalyst for their spirited talents. Judy told me, "One farmer grows fifteen varieties of daffodils. Another wonderful man we know collects things in the woods for us: beehives, abandoned birds' nests, mosses and lichens, bittersweet and anything else he finds. We're never sure when he'll come into the shop, but when he does, it's magical. Ladies are always growing sweet peas and gladiolus, and other summer flowers in their gardens for us. I guess it's because we all share so much in this small town that our shop has such a warm atmosphere and magical spirit."

Minimum: None, and no charge for in-town delivery
Credit cards: MasterCard and VISA

MINNEAPOLIS

Larkspur
WENDY COGGINS AND SCOTT REHOVSKY

122 North Fourth Street
Minneapolis, MN 55402
(612) 332-2140

Those of you who live in or near Minneapolis are probably already familiar with Wendy's wonderful free-lance work with dried flowers and may recognize Scott from Silver Swans. Although they've been collaborating on projects for several years, they just recently formally combined their talents by opening Larkspur.

They describe their work as ranging from Old World to romantic country-garden arrangements. Always on hand are wreaths, topiaries of dried materials or fresh flowers, Dutch flower balls and baskets decorated on the outside with a combination of dried and fresh flowers.

Gifts and accessories include antique vases, Italian terracotta and papier-mâché animals and angels that are decorated with dried flowers, gilded, painted or given a combination of treatments. Their innovative "sleeping" pillows, made of chintz or moiré and filled with a sachet of herbs meant to induce sleep, are very popular.

Minimum: $35.00 plus delivery
Credit to be arranged
Also serves: Bloomington and St. Paul

Secret Gardens
GINNY STRONG, LLOP

1705 James Avenue, S
Minneapolis, MN 55403
(612) 374-3739

Ginny is a free-lancer whose background includes planning estate flower and vegetable gardens and owning a retail flower shop. "Now that I no longer own a shop, I get to fool around and experiment more," she says. "Things would get so hectic at the store that I often felt my talents were going to waste." Ginny's following is so demanding that often she must refer requests to her friends in the business.

For her daily work she creates massed bouquets with an emphasis on the flower. Her arrangements are full and sophisticated, though she can accommodate the loose and airy look as well. Gift arrangements are set in baskets, interior-glazed terracotta or simple glass cylinders. She combines garden flowers with Holland imports and a surprise touch of more unusual materials she's gathered from the fields.

Minimum: $50.00
24-hour notice required
Best at market
Credit to be arranged
Also serves: Minneapolis only, not St. Paul

Wisteria Design Studio Ltd.
RUSSELL TOSCANO

3120 West 28th Street
Minneapolis, MN 55416
(612) 925-9470

Russell came out to Minnesota two years ago from New York, and he's now doing some of the best work in the Minneapolis–St. Paul area. His signature look is clean and contemporary, incorporating many tropicals and giving foliage center stage—not the overused sprengerii ferns or lemon leaves, but bold, handsome ti leaves, sago palm or heliconia leaves. Russell says, "I love using bamboo. It gives such a great upward lift to the piece." He and his talented associates never use oasis, only clear water. When they need a structure in a vase, they submerge natural reed and twist it, forming a mechanism that holds the flower stems in place.

At Wisteria the vases are as important as the flowers. The focal point often starts at the neck of the vase with an attention-grabbing flower such as a king protea or a marvelous orchid. From there the eye travels downward as well as upward, so that the container takes on an important significance in the overall presentation.

A real treat of Russell's is the way he presents a dozen roses. They come wrapped in ti leaves, like a large pouch, and are tied off with raffia. When you untie the raffia, the whole thing unfolds by itself, and you have a wonderful display of roses backed by a spray of handsome foliage. Easy to carry and easy to place in a vase, this unique method of sending roses has become so popular that many people ask him to air express it (which he can do only in warm weather).

Minimum: $35.00 plus delivery
Credit to be arranged
Also serves: Bloomington and St. Paul

MISSISSIPPI

BILOXI

Coastal Floral Design: Keesler Airforce Shops
RON WILKINSON

P.O. Box 5036
Biloxi, MS 39534
(601) 435-2543

At twenty-seven years of age, Ron seems young for such an enormous talent that covers a wide spectrum of styles. His contemporary work betrays a strong Oriental influence. Otherwise everything he creates is soft and natural, breezy and airy. He uses a lot of "sticks": wing-tip elm, white birch, grapevines, blossoming fruit trees, forsythia and quince. The list is endless; and when combined with home-grown roses and Holland imports, the effect is startlingly exquisite.

Minimum: $20.00 plus delivery
All major credit cards
Also serves: Gulfport

CLARKSDALE

Moreland-Price Florist
BETTY WALTON

P.O. Box 505
Clarksdale, MS 38614
(601) 624-6556

So what does Moreland-Price have to do with Betty Walton? No, she didn't buy an existing

136

business; she named the store after her two grandmothers, to make it sound as though the shop has been around for a long time.

Betty imports flowers and mixes them with those she grows herself in "a great big garden out back." She says of her garden, "Oh, it just looks terrible all the time, because I'm always rummaging around cutting this or that." She places coreopsis and dill comfortably in glass bubbles with Holland imports or artfully combines potted plants in baskets with cuts, "so people have something to keep when the cuts die. I love planting violets with variegated ivy and adding cut lilies or freesia," she says.

She made a name for herself by wrapping old Coke bottles in moss, tying them off with raffia and filling them with flowers, weeds and other wonderful things from her garden. After all, Coca-Cola started in the South so perhaps only Southerners know what real Coke is all about! Needless to say, it's ideas like these that keep costs down.

Minimum: $10.00 plus delivery
All major credit cards

COLUMBIA

Flowers Unlimited
Matt Wood, AIFD

518 South High School Avenue
Columbia, MS 39429
(601) 736-8717

In the very small towns of the Deep South one usually does the best one can. Columbia is lucky to have Matt Wood. He has a garden out back to help him keep his inventory interesting, but during the winter a hundred white carnations or a dozen lilies are a good idea.

When Matt has the luxury of choosing from the outdoors, natural arrangements are delivered in baskets and are often combined with jellies, potpourri or candy, leaving the recipient with something once the flowers are gone. Last Thanksgiving homemade breads were combined with flowers, for a touch of warmth.

Minimum: $20.00 plus delivery
Credit cards: MasterCard and VISA

JACKSON

Posh Flowers
MARK FOSHEE AND FREDERICK AND CYNTHIA BRIGGS

1060 East County Line Road
Ridgeland, MS 39157
(601) 956-2423

Although its designers can create works from the avant-garde to the traditional, one of Posh's signature arrangements is a homemade vase that looks like a tree trunk. It's a glass cylinder with bark and lichen or mosses glued to it. Into it goes a handful of unadulterated Mississippi weeds combined with garden roses or lilies or whatever the customer likes. And, Mark adds, "I love to use sunflowers." The result is wildly romantic.

Mark, Frederick and Cynthia are multitalented, so just let them know what you want. For children or a party they splatter paint on watercolor paper, which they use to "ribbon wrap" their vases. Instead of bud vases, Posh will dip a water tube with fresh flowers into a bag of potpourri. "It's so much nicer than having yet another bud vase to put under your sink," says Cynthia.

Minimum: $20.00 plus delivery
All major credit cards

LAUREL

Merritt's Florist and Gifts
JOHN MERRITT

North Laurel Shopping Center
Laurel, MS 39440
(601) 426-9016

Although John is very capable of working in a contemporary manner, his day-to-day creations are European with a cozy country feeling. His customers are concerned with color-coordinating their flowers with the rooms they go into. "Our big colors are those from pink to rose, and white," John told me. "We do very little in orange or yellow. There's just not much call for the Caribbean colors in Laurel."

He uses a lot of native foliage: magnolia, boxwood, *Camellia sasanqua* and, especially, elaeagnus. "That's great for upward motion in large arrangements," John says. He also uses imports.

Minimum: $25.00; no delivery charge within the city limits
All major credit cards
Also serves: Ellisville and Heidelberg

OXFORD

Oxford Floral
BETTE AND JEFF BUTLER

P.O. Box 519
Oxford, MS 38655
(601) 234-2515

Talent abounds in this college-town shop. Although Bette and Jeff have won professional floral competitions in the South, they focus on the natural beauty of flowers and the requirements of the customer. Typically flowers are combined loosely in baskets, clear glass or ceramic containers crafted by local artisans. Another favorite is a clean and simple display in the style of Ronaldo Maia (see the shop by that name under New York City): bud vases with just a few stems in each scattered up and down a long table.

Minimum: $20.00 plus delivery
All major credit cards

TUPELO

❖➤➤❭❬❬❬❖

Flowers By Jody
JODY BISHOP, AIFD

728 South Gloster
Tupelo, MS 38801
(601) 844-9298

A variety of native foliage and Holland imports is whimsically combined to create a woodsy or garden effect in many of Jody Bishop's arrangements. While out hunting with his son, Jody collects driftwood, mosses, red birch and cattails. In the summer equisetum, magnolia and Johnsongrass are abundant. Johnsongrass, a four- to five-foot weed with a tiny seed cone on top, is effective in flower arrangements but an infuriating pest to farmers. Every southern farmer knows how this weed spreads rampantly through fields by underground rhizomes, and how difficult it is to control. Finally, Jody has found one redeeming use for it—and finds like this are what great florists are all about.

Arrangements go out in wicker baskets, glass cylinders or terra-cotta trays. The shop has exclusive rights to a line of unglazed sandstone pottery with ripples of color through it, made by southern Mississippi artists. The pieces come in all sorts of shapes, from salad-bowl sizes to platters, and they're surprisingly inexpensive.

Holidays are an opportunity for Jody and his staff to create clever, unusual and attractive gifts, so be sure to ask about them.

Minimum: $20.00 plus delivery
All major credit cards

MISSOURI

KANSAS CITY

The Absolute Florist
LEROY MILLER, AIFD, AND LORI OWENS

546 Westport Road
Kansas City, MO 64111
(816) 931-8582

Leroy and Lori are known for their clean, dramatic, very contemporary work. They do beautiful strong-line designs incorporating unusual tropicals such as rare heliconias and tulip anthuriums. With the addition of inorganic props such as Mylar, glitter stick, or Plexiglas, these arrangements can achieve a very sculptural look. Leroy and Lori also do loose, stylized European bouquets combining Holland imports such as lilies, freesia, tulips and roses. "Our European arrangements are not English," says Leroy, "because they are not casual or frilly. Instead, similar colors and flowers are grouped into a perceptible design." They are fortunate to have access to seasonal garden roses and wildflowers as well.

Flower-related giftware is displayed in a gallery-like setting. A collection of clay pots, glazed with gilt or other *faux* finishes, is grouped on one side of the shop. Beautiful but reasonably priced dried topiaries on curly willow trunks stand together on the other side. Unusual bromeliad plants and orchids highlight opposing corners of the store. The choice of containers and decorative accessories is extensive, ranging in price from five dollars to five hundred. In-house holiday designs are available as well. For Valentine's Day, heart-shaped terra-cotta containers filled with roses were available in different sizes and prices.

What keeps this sophisticated shop from being intimidating are Lori and Leroy's inviting friendliness and flexible service.

Minimum: $30.00 plus delivery
All major credit cards
Also serves: In Kansas: Shawnee Mission

Trapp & Company
ROBERT D. TRAPP

208 Westport Road
Kansas City, MO 64111
(816) 931-6940

The design team in this shop is terrifically versatile and capable of displaying a wide range of floral talent, from high-tech contemporary to baskets of wildflowers. A large selection of tropicals, Holland flowers and blooming plants are available daily.

But what's most exciting is the innovative and tasteful ideas the designers create: topiaries made from their own pomanders, which are attached to a trunk of bunched cinnamon sticks and set in terra-cotta; the custom line of balustrade vases already painted or made to order; and fabulous baskets whose rims are composed of masses of dried flowers.

As with all great design teams, presentation is as important as the arrangement itself, and Trapp & Company is always developing unexpected juxtapositions. Upon request they will surround an arrangement with the appropriate picture frames—gilt rococo, English walnut or country pine. This concept took hold with their clientele after Trapp's designers created an Old World arrangement for an art benefit; a four- by six-foot gilt Baroque frame surrounded a huge Flemish arrangement, set in a fabulous urn—a three-dimensional Huysum. Indeed, art is alive at Trapp & Company.

Minimum: $35.00 plus delivery
All major credit cards
Also serves: In Kansas, Shawnee Mission

SAINT LOUIS

Ken Miesner's
KEN MIESNER

292 Plaza Frontenac
St. Louis, MO 63131
(314) 567-6650

Ken Miesner's name is synonymous with quality: A distinct quality of design sets his work apart from that of the crowd. Bright anemones coming out of a fresh pear and pink roses mixed with cabbages are examples of Ken's surprising touches, which are combined with the finest in contemporary and traditional looks.

Christmas is a special time for Ken, who also owns a year-round Christmas shop, so expect anything from elegant bouquets of rubrum lilies with soft hemlock to whimsical candy baskets.

Minimum: $25.00 plus delivery
All major credit cards
Also serves: Chesterfield, Clayton, Frontenac, Ladue and University City

Jon Prel
JON PREL

401 North Euclid
St. Louis, MO 63108
(314) 367-4300

Jon Prel's favorite direction from a customer is "I don't care what you do, just make it fabulous."

And you can believe he will. He uses lots of flowers while maintaining a strong respect for the space between them. His work is somewhat architectural and contemporary, but not contrived.

He is famous for his windows, especially his "Easter Nuns," who show up in every Easter on a bicycle, each year wearing a different habit and sporting yet another fabulous Jon Prel arrangement in the basket on the handlebars.

Minimum: $25.00 plus delivery
All major credit cards
Also serves: Chesterfield, Clayton, Frontenac, Ladue and University City

MONTANA

BILLINGS

Gainan's
CHARLES, MICHAEL AND ELIZABETH GAINAN

502 North 30th Street
Great Falls, MT 59101
(406) 245-6434

You can get just about anything you want from the shop, greenhouse and outdoor nursery that make up this expansive operation. From herb planters and blooming, foliage and bedding plants, to fresh arrangements and all sorts of exciting gifts, Gainan's has it all. With a business this large, be sure you speak with a designer when placing your order. Arrangements are typically loose, natural and gardeny, but high-style designs are often featured in the cooler.

The extensive choice of gifts includes Paperwhite linens, Adirondack-style chairs and tables, Italian porcelains and terra-cotta, southwestern-style pottery, antiques, various potpourris and lots of dried flowers and wreaths. Gainan's is an oasis of taste and style in the middle of the West. The Gainans' reputation carries them to many neighboring states to design and implement creative themes for ranch parties.

Minimum: $15.00 plus delivery
All major credit cards

BOZEMAN

❧➤➤✕⧲⧲

Langohr's Flowerland
STEVEN AND MARYANN LIEBMAN

P.O. Box 306
Bozeman, MT 59715
(406) 587-4407

A very traditional approach to flower arranging is taken here, so if you want cut flowers, be specific and send something simple like a mass of daisies or alstroemeria lilies in a clear glass bowl tied with ribbon or raffia. But you'll find many exciting choices among the plants growing in the Liebmans' greenhouses. It is here that you should focus your requests for gifts. Steve's extensive horticultural interests inspire him to grow many unusual blooming plants such as calla lilies, gerberas, tulips, iris, paper-white narcissus, stargazer lilies, and amaryllis. You'll find large geraniums, annuals such as snapdragons and zinnias and perennials such as delphinium, foxglove and liatris. Decorative herbs like thyme, oregano and dill are grown here as well. Just ask what's in season and what looks good. Containers include plain or Italian terra-cotta pots, baskets and other decorator pots.

Minimum: $20.00 plus delivery
All major credit cards
Also serves: Big Sky and West Yellowstone

MISSOULA

Bitterroot Flower Shop
DAVID DAVIES

811 South Higgins
Missoula, MT 59801
(406) 542-0309

Four years ago David bought this traditional shop and revamped it with flowers he imports daily from all over the world. These are displayed in handsome baskets in a market-type setting, making them very accessible. He also keeps a wide selection of foliage and blooming plants.

David has a keen marketing spirit, and often takes the lead by promoting a flower that may be common to residents of San Francisco or New York but not well known in Missoula. Slowly but surely his customers become accustomed to the new variety, and enough demand develops to warrant stocking the soon-to-be-popular flower. The end result? An inspiring range of fresh choice at Bitterroot.

David also stocks an assortment of containers made from different materials: wicker, ceramic, brass, clear glass and terracotta. The versatile designers here can execute just about any type of arrangement. Creative solutions are often developed for holiday gifts. For last Mother's Day an affordable gift for children to give their moms was thoughtfully inspired: Tiny baskets were filled with minicarnations and a single lollipop. Sweet and sensitive!

Minimum: $20.00 plus delivery, which is determined on a case-by-case basis
Credit cards: MasterCard and VISA

A country arrangement of meadow flowers, grasses and summer annuals and perennials, including zinnias, sunflowers, pokeweed, gooseneck lysimachia, 'Silver King' artemisia, September gentian and hydrangea.

Florist: VSF, New York, NY

Photographer: Elizabeth Watt

A selection of standard topiaries, including ivy, myrtle, rosemary and variegated myrtle. The pink flower at right is bougainvillea.

Florist: VSF, New York, NY
Photographer: Elizabeth Watt

A striking contemporary arrangement of three pendulous hibiscus flowers dangling from schefflera leaves, one tangerine heliconia and an orange ginger with its stem wrapped in spathiphyllum leaves. A papyrus flower is punctuated with papyrus canes and spathiphyllum leaves. At the lip of the container are fiddlehead ferns with a Posh adaptation of a hibiscus stamen in an orchid flower.

Florist: Posh Flowers, Jackson, MS
Photographer: Tom Joynt

A swath of spring
flowers and herbs
from the perennial
border in a free-
flowing cottage-
garden-style arrange-
ment. Flowers include
peonies, bearded iris,
columbine, bleeding
heart, lupine, roses,
a poppy, flowering
thyme, penstemon,
lavender, lady's-
mantle, sage, lamb's-
ears, garden helio-
trope, various ferns
and curly willow.

Florist: Flower
Hill Farm,
Williamsburg, MA
Photographer:
Carol Duke

A fragrant Victorian bouquet combining analogous colors of freesia, roses, sweet peas and lilac.

Florist: John Hoover, Memphis, TN
Photographer: Mary Wallace Crocker

A full-blown Flemish bouquet of eratum lilies, pink rambling roses, peonies, bearded iris, parrot tulips, columbine, Queen Anne's lace, sprays of red epidendrum orchids and dill.

Florist: Mädderlake, New York, NY
Photographer: Langdon Clay

A landscape of spring flowers: yellow ranunculus, yellow-centered orange poppies, columbine, Queen Anne's lace, white daisies, maidenhair fern, purple scilla, tangerine and yellow gerbera daisies, pink nerine lilies and grape hyacinth punctuated with bear grass and held in a low, mossed container lit with votive candles in bird's nests.

Florist: The Flower Basket, Westport, CT
Photographer: Nancy MacFarland

A tablescape of tropical flowers in contemporary containers that can be used individually or, as shown, in a grouping. Yellow protea with its own foliage and decorative okra with a touch of curly willow branch occupy the vase at left. Three single red heliconia are in chrome vials. At right is a mixed bouquet of kangaroo paws, red protea, caladium leaves and the tubular insectivore, the pitcher-plant.

Florist: The Flower Basket, Westport, CT
Photographer: Martin Tornallyay

NEBRASKA

LINCOLN

Hillis, The Florist
MIKE HILLIS

13th and M Streets
Lincoln, NE 68508
(402) 474-2333

Sixty to eighty varieties of flowers, plus a combination of locally grown perennials, wildflowers and imports from all over the world fill this shop. Mike's personal greenhouse is teeming with blooming perennial plants, lots of bulb plants and a surprising variety of topiaries, including ones made from scented geranium, thyme, lantana and rosemary. The styles created here range from full, romantic bouquets to high-style minimalist arrangements.

The gift line is horticulturally related: blackamoors holding glass vials, lots and lots of books on gardening and flowers, baskets, terra-cotta containers and clear glass vases. When I find a shop filled with as much talent and taste as this one, my best advice is to explore what Mike and his associates are excited about at the moment, make a choice and leave the rest to them.

Minimum: $30.00 plus delivery
All major credit cards

OMAHA

Piccolo's
FRANK PICCOLO

2504 South 132nd Court
Omaha, NE 68144
(402) 334-6890

Several years ago Frank decided to transform his shop and began to specialize in Hawaiian tropicals and Holland imports. His expertise covers both ends of the design spectrum: "We see very little in between the two extremes of high-tech contemporary and English-garden design," says Frank. "But whatever we're doing, it's as important to be artistic and honest as it is to be new and innovative." His contemporary designs are often punctuated with glitter stick or various colors of Mylar. And for his English bouquets, which are loose and airy, Mike makes use of imported garden flowers.

Containers range from ceramic pots and clear glass vases to grapevine baskets and Italian terra-cotta pots. Blooming plants are the usual azaleas, kalanchoe and geraniums; however, Frank does have access to foliage plants and unusual topiaries.

For holidays, he and his associates create clever decorative pieces. For example, one Easter he secured an attractive three-foot branch in a mossed base and decorated it with all kinds of tiny ornaments, primarily miniature wooden Easter eggs that were festively painted. A similar idea was used for Christmas, using live two-foot evergreen trees with miniature lights, miniature garlands and every kind of miniature Christmas ornament they could find. You can be as specific as you want to, within reason, and Frank and his associates will more than adequately satisfy your needs.

Minimum: $25.00 plus delivery
All major credit cards

NEVADA

CARSON CITY

Our Flower Shop
MARGARET AND JOHN McGOODWIN

602 East John Street
Carson City, NV 89706
(702) 883-7744

This mother-and-son team strives to please the customer with a combination of versatility and value. Although they are capable of anything, they prefer doing big, full, romantic arrangements packed with lots of different flowers, reflecting a Victorian aesthetic.

The shop is in a turn-of-the-century townhouse with dramatic twelve-foot ceilings. Columns separate the two front parlors, and an inviting fireplace roars during the winter. "You can imagine, with this kind of setting, that Christmas is a very exciting holiday for us," says Margaret. "We decorate the entire house."

Seasonal blooming plants are available such as cyclamen and potted lilies, paper-whites and tulips. The desert climate, with daily temperature swings of forty degrees, precludes growing anything locally, so all flowers are shipped in. Tropicals need to be ordered specially, in advance. Give Johnny and Margaret the basic parameters of color and container choice and leave the details to them.

Minimum: $20.00 plus delivery
All major credit cards

LAS VEGAS

A French Bouquet
BOB WERNER

2121 East Tropicana Avenue
Las Vegas, NV 89119
(702) 739-8484

Diana Ross accurately described Bob Werner when she told him, "I don't know anybody who can arrange a $250 bouquet as quickly as you can and answer the phone at the same time." Bob is big time. He has organized some of the biggest parties and conventions ever, and it's true—he still answers his own phone. You don't go through switchboards and secretaries to talk to him. It's admirable to see somebody stay as close to the everyday aspects of a business as Bob does, especially when he has every excuse to slip into managing from afar. Undoubtedly that's why he's maintained such a stellar clientele over the last twenty-seven years. He's hands on and quality-conscious.

Because of the remarkable business he does, Bob has a great reputation with the wholesalers and can get just about any material you want. He runs his own trucks out of the LA markets and buys directly from people all over the world. Be sure to tell him what you want, since he is capable of just about everything.

Minimum: $25.00 plus delivery
All major credit cards

RENO

La Fleur
FRANK GRAVES, AIFD

475 South Arlington
Reno, NV 89501
(702) 322-8666

It's evident that Frank's love of gardening inspires his floral aesthetic. If left up to him, an arrangement from La Fleur is an opulent bouquet filled with flowers shipped in from all over the world. But Frank can take advantage of anything with aesthetic possibility. He cites one example: "There's a pear tree in my yard whose fruits have never enjoyed full maturity. When the fruits are just about two inches big, I cut as many branches as I can. The leafy branches with their pendulous fruits are perfect for arranging!" Daily arrangements are done in your choice of a basket, clear glass vase or terra-cotta container.

Frank creates lovely planted compositions with blooming gardenias, hibiscus, orchids, hyacinths, or lilies of the valley— anything that is in season and unusual. Whatever you order here, your selection is in the best of hands.

Minimum: $35.00 plus delivery
All major credit cards

NEW HAMPSHIRE

HANOVER

Evergreen
MARY BUTLER

West Lebanon Plaza
West Lebanon, NH 03784
(603) 298-5009

Mary is always looking for ways to express her imaginative talents, but her first love is arranging garden flowers in a lovely natural, loose manner. Realizing that the character and quality of the flowers must guide her creative spirit, she goes to market herself and handpicks the flowers she then combines with locally grown, seasonal garden flowers and herbs. Gorgeous, fragrant spring bouquets include white delphinium clumped with raspberry-colored peonies, sprays of old-fashioned roses, white lilac and freesia. Tropicals are by special order. "Most of my work goes out in baskets, however I strongly encourage glass because the flowers last so much longer in plain water rather than oasis," says Mary.

The shop is filled with wonderful terra-cotta containers, Paperwhite linens and laces, potpourri and soaps from Crabtree & Evelyn, fabric-covered hatboxes and picture frames, and loads of gardening books. Orchids are seasonally available. Blooming plants are nestled throughout the shop and often used to create lush, romantic planted baskets. If you order a basket or terra-cotta planter filled with seasonal herbs, a card written in calligraphy explains how to use and care for them. When appropriate, the historical symbolism of the particular herb is told as well. There's lots of tasteful style here, so give the minimal guidelines and leave the details to Mary and her associates.

Minimum: $25.00 plus delivery
All major credit cards
Also serves: In Vermont: Norwich and White River Junction

KEENE

Greens and Things
MARION AND CAROL RAYNOR

Colony Mill Market Place
222 West Street
Keene, NH 03431
(603) 357-1506

Lots of good, though commercial, ideas abound here, from "The Butterfly Mug" for Secretary's Week to "The European Bouquet" for Mother's Day. In the words of Mrs. Raynor, "To expand and stay ahead, you do everything: flowers, plants, gifts and balloons, and in all styles, from vegetative to ikebana to parallelism." Flowers are imported from all over the world, arriving six days a week, so you know that the inventory is always fresh. And you know what to expect, from Dutch tulips, lilies and freesias to Hawaiian tropicals and South American carnations, chrysanthemums and daisies. Nothing is derived from local gardens.

The designer's attention to detail is evident in the arrangements here; a good deal of respect is given to technical skills. Go with a well-executed design or simply a great big bunch of fresh flowers.

Minimum: $15.00 plus delivery
All major credit cards
Also serves: Marlboro, Spofford and Swanzey

MANCHESTER

Alluring Creations
NORM BELANGER

152 Bridge Street
Manchester, NH 03104
(603) 668-3022

Styles at Alluring Creations range from high-style contemporary or lush European to plain everyday colonial bouquets, but Norm most enjoys the strong-line contemporary work. He uses carefully selected tropical flowers, adding garden-type blooms when the two complement one another. Norm believes people are inspired to use him after seeing one of his high-style creations displayed in the shop window.

Most of his daily work goes out in glass unless you specify a basket. All of his flowers are gathered from wholesalers, including assorted blooming and foliage plants; nothing is locally grown. Keep your plans simple and be straightforward about what you want. Norm is more than willing to do what his customers prefer.

Minimum: $20.00 plus delivery
All major credit cards
Also serves: Auburn, Bedford and Hooksett

PETERBOROUGH

Greens and Things
MARION AND CAROL RAYNOR

Peterborough Plaza
Peterborough, NH 03458
(603) 924-9291

Similar to Marion and Carol's shop in Keene. See entry for Greens and Things, above.

PORTSMOUTH

D. L. Browne
DAVID BROWNE

865 Islington Street
Portsmouth, NH 03801
(603) 436-6653

David refers to his arrangements as "character statements," explaining that "we strive to send flowers that reflect our customer's personality. I ask questions about them, and their answers stimulate my creativity." While David's arrangements do comply with the personality of the recipient, he sets his limits within the realm of good taste. His skills traverse the design spectrum, from contemporary high-style arrangements to English country bouquets. You can be assured that whatever genre he's working in, the flowers always take center stage, and the inherent form of each one is graciously respected.

He imports his flowers from all over the world but also takes advantage of local gardens. "In the summer our inventory is almost 80 percent garden flowers: delphiniums, lupines, bleeding heart, lilies, salvia and lots of herbs. In fact I'll use any plant for it's foliage or flower as long as it has merit," says David. More often than not, arrangements go out in clear glass, but there is a large selection of handsome baskets as well.

The presentation of David's arrangements is noteworthy. Each one is prepared as though it comes from one of the finest shops on Madison Avenue. It is placed in a box and fluffed inside and out with tissue paper of a coordinating color; then the whole thing is wrapped again in cellophane and tied at the top with color-coordinated curly ribbons.

Minimum: $30.00 plus delivery
All major credit cards

SEABROOK

Jasmine's Flower Shoppe
DEBRA A. DEFREZE

779 Lafayette Road
Heritage Village
Seabrook, NH 03874
(603) 474-3020

Debra describes her work as "a soft version of contemporary; progressive without hard lines." Tropicals are massed in large bouquets much as the English mass together garden flowers. For the most part Debra's arrangements are unconstructed, with a pleasing, natural palette. Nevertheless, schooled influences are evident in her work.

Up to forty different kinds of fresh imported garden flowers, as well as lots of locally grown seasonal perennials and annuals, are displayed in clear glass cylinders around the store. Tropicals must be special-ordered.

Herb baskets are seasonally available, and the shop stocks inexpensive table wines and champagnes to send along with flowers. A nice selection of blooming plants is also available. Debra creates lovely hand-tied European bouquets that go out wrapped in crisp clear cellophane and tied with ribbons. Whatever your sensibility, be specific about what you want.

Minimum: $20.00 plus delivery
All major credit cards
Also serves: In Massachusetts: Newburyport; in New Hampshire: Hampton and Rye

NEW JERSEY

FAR HILLS

Larkspur & Thyme
CAROL MAGADINI
Route 1
Far Hills, NJ 07931
(201) 879-7014

Carol's artistic arrangements vary with the seasons. Spring, summer and fall flowers are taken from huge cutting gardens of herbs, perennials and wildflowers and casually, though artfully combined with imports. Foxglove, campanulas, delphiniums, cosmos, wild asters, alchemilla (lady's-mantle), lavender, rosemary and many unusual herbs complement these arrangements. In wintertime she likes mounds of roses mixed with scented geraniums cut from her greenhouse stock.

Planted perennial baskets are one of Carol's most popular items. In bold grapevine baskets she'll mix coralbells, campanulas, and foxglove with thyme or other herbs edged in. Although expensive, the charm of this sort of gift is that the perennials can be planted in the garden after their blooms have been enjoyed indoors or on a porch.

Minimum: $40.00 plus delivery
24-hour notice required
Credit to be arranged
Also serves: Bernardsville, Morristown, New Vernon and Oldwick

Wildfields
LIZA KOVEN

Dickson's Mill Road
Green Village, NJ 07935
(201) 377-9061

Liza's work varies in size from huge arrangements of flowering branches combined with spring flowers or swatches of autumn leaves and asters to cozy but dramatic baskets of cultivated wildflowers.

When not arranging flowers she's painting portraits in oils. "It's from my fine-arts background that I have developed a great feeling for the nuances of color, and I've combined that with a nurtured sensibility for balance and harmony in design," she says. "I've always got my eyes peeled for that perfect vine or special branch growing in the wild or in my own garden."

Minimum: $40.00 plus delivery
48-hour notice required
Credit to be arranged
Also serves: Bernardsville, Madison, Morristown and Summit

MONTCLAIR

Mary McGeown Flowers "By Special Arrangement"
MARY MCGEOWN

28 South Fullerton Avenue
Montclair, NJ 07042
(201) 764-7496

Since she's a good friend and an admirer of Sheila Macqueen's, it's understandable that Mary combines a traditional English elegance with her own natural flair. Although her work is not daring or artsy, it is full of life and movement. Fully blown white garden roses are combined with ivy and cranberries for a centerpiece. Red roses, spruce and protea are poised on the mantle for Christmas.

Mary imports many of her flowers, but also has many grown specially for her, including garden roses, herbs, perennials and annuals. Like many people who dislike certain flowers that are at odds with their particular style, Mary shies away from liatris, anthuriums and common filler flowers such as baby's breath.

Her favorite containers are baskets, be they silver, glass, porcelain, wicker, painted or wire. Nevertheless, she keeps a selection of glass vases and wonderful antique containers she's scavenged in various shops on her travels.

Minimum: $35.00 plus delivery
Credit to be arranged

NEWARK

Arcadia
JO AND ELLIE COVIELLO

577 Broad Street
Newark, NJ 07102
(201) 622-6283

Located in downtown Newark, Arcadia caters to many professional and commercial clients as well as private ones. Here, the focus is decidedly on the flowers. Neither time nor energy is wasted on gift items or plants. They will do exactly what the customer wants with whatever kinds of flowers he or she chooses. "Whatever you want, whatever you like, we can get," quips Jo. And he means it, so be very specific about what you want and how you want it presented. Jo and his staff are pleasantly matter-of-fact, and aesthetically minded but with a sharp eye for efficiency.

Minimum: $25.00 plus delivery
All major credit cards

PRINCETON

by Design
JUDITH RULON-MILLER AND CARROLL BEVER

P.O. Box 431
Kingston, NJ 08528
(609) 921-1076/-0032

Rhythm and clean lines, with nothing fussy or contrived, are the hallmark of the designs here. Dutch imports and garden flowers are arranged to exhibit their natural grace, creating a light and airy effect. Carroll and Judy's work is sophisticated and unpretentious, in the Mädderlake style (see listing under New York City). Flowers are often arranged in clear glass, as the stems play an important role in the overall design, but baskets will be used upon request.

"It's hard to improve on nature, which is why we pick from the wild as well as from the garden," says Judy. "We tend to keep our flowers compatible by choosing material to reflect the changing seasons. In other words, tulips are not arranged with chrysanthemums, since they don't bloom at the same time of year."

By Design does not make deliveries to hospitals.

Minimum: $35.00 plus delivery
24-hour notice required
Credit to be arranged
Also serves: Hopewell, Lawrenceville and other small towns within a 20-mile radius of Princeton

Flowers by Ginny Miller
GINNY MILLER

Mountain View, Box 57
Blawenburg, NJ 08504
(609) 466-2691

In the last five years that Ginny has been free-lancing, her reputation has spread rapidly by word of mouth. Her work space, in an eighteenth-century wagon shed, is very English in feeling. Her clients love the atmosphere and often stop by just to chat and relax. In the spring, when her gardens are blooming with color and fragrance, Ginny sets out tables covered with Victorian chintz and has tea for her regular customers. This is probably the closest she comes to advertising.

"Although I try to satisfy all tastes in flowers, I most enjoy English-garden country arrangements in dark baskets," Ginny says. She receives fresh shipments of flowers daily from Holland, but always incorporates something from her own garden.

Due to a limited amount of space, she rarely carries foliage or blooming plants during the colder months, though she usually has them available when the weather gets warmer.

Minimum: $35.00 plus delivery
Prefers 24-hour notice, but can handle emergencies
Credit cards: MasterCard and VISA
Also serves: Hopewell, Montgomery Township and Princeton

RUMSON

Living Windows
MARTHA CHAMBERLAIN AND ANN TARLTON

105 East River Road
Rumson, NJ 07760
(201) 842-0021

Tasteful English-style bouquets are custom-created here. Imported flowers are combined with seasonal garden flowers grown by Ann and Martha or by local gardeners. Magnolia, lilacs, flowering fruit branches, fritillaria, wood hyacinth and decorative herbs such as dill, marjoram and basil are some of the local flora they take advantage of. They don't carry tropicals on a daily basis but will special-order them. "We like to know the occasion and spot in the home that the bouquet is meant for. That way we can be sure to send the appropriate size and shape arrangement. And of course, color preference is crucial," says Ms. Chamberlain.

The choice of gifts is tempting, from small hand-painted baskets to antique Chinese vases. One of their most popular containers is a basket with chintz bows and swags, the fabric of which has been custom-starched and clear-varnished to hold its cheerful shape and color. Unless one of their special containers is chosen, daily arrangements are prepared in clear glass or baskets. Dried wreaths and topiaries are made in-house also.

There's a tremendous selection of orchids and blooming plants; however, no balloons, foliage plants or fruit.

Minimum: $35.00 plus delivery
Credit cards: MasterCard and VISA
Also serves: Fair Haven, Little Silver, Locust, Middletown, Red Bank and Sea Bright

TRENTON

Makrancy's Floral Shop, Garden Center & Greenhouse
JOSEPH AND MAGGIE MAKRANCY

966 Kuser Road
Trenton, NJ 08619
(609) 587-2543

"Stems are the going thing right now in flower arranging," says Mr. Makrancy, referring to the loose garden bouquets that are displayed in clear glass. Nevertheless, the six designers that work here are capable of anything and are encouraged to strike their own balance between a customer's request and the aesthetic possibilities of the flowers. After all, it's this kind of respectful autonomy that keeps good designers around and nurtures their individual talents. The flowers they work with are shipped in mostly from Hawaii and Holland, however they do have access to locally grown field perennials and annuals, from sunflowers to hybrid tea roses.

The big treat here is what Mr. Makrancy grows in his seven greenhouses: foliage plants, seasonal holiday specialties from poinsettias to Easter lilies, and wonderful bedding plants in the summer and spring. Martha Washington geraniums—soft pink or white with blooms that look like rhododendron blossoms—make a great gift for the pool or porch when potted in terra-cotta with vinca or candytuft. Orchids are plentiful and so are herb plants for planted compositions. Just ask what's perfect and ready from the greenhouse.

The shop is filled with loads of gifts, from porcelain swans to little bunnies in papier-mâché. Shaker-style antiques in pine and oak, and a renowned collection of antique sleighs, are the highlights of the gift selection. Take advantage of the designers' receptivity and inventiveness; give them an idea of what you want, then set them loose to create.

Minimum: $25.00 plus delivery
All major credit cards
Also serves: Mantoloking and Princeton

NEW MEXICO

ALBUQUERQUE

Silver Petal
GARY MARTOGLIO

14 Fashion Square
100 San Mateo, NE
Albuquerque, NM 87110
(505) 262-0995

Although this shop is only a year old, its proprietor has been involved in all aspects of the flower business for fifteen years and feels very comfortable in his present position. Gary says, "The key is, I love it." From traditional gardeny arrangements to exotic tropicals, he's got a lot to offer, and he's very value conscious. He believes that "things can look great and don't have to be composed of a lot of expensive flowers."

One of his most popular gifts is a perfume-bottle bud vase that he has specially blown for his shop. The inside vial is usually a soft pastel and is surrounded by a larger clear glass bubble. Although it's expensive, it's perfect for any setting. He also carries his own potpourri. Undoubtedly, Gary will set new standards for Albuquerque.

With specific direction, Gary and his associates produce dependable work.

Minimum: $25.00 plus delivery
Credit cards: MasterCard and VISA

SANTA FE

Canyon Road Flowers
Jon Gurrola

423 Canyon Road
Santa Fe, NM 87501
(505) 983-9785

Driven by a lifelong love for flowers, Jon quit a successful career as an electrical engineer five years ago to open Canyon Road Flowers. His reputation was quickly established, and his clients have been so satisfied with his work that they often ask him to travel all over the country to do parties and weddings for them in their hometowns.

Jon's imported flowers blend easily with locally grown perennials and herbs. Santa Fe's climate lends itself to growing the kinds of flowers you find in such temperate states as Virginia and Pennsylvania. The range of seasonal choice is inspiring.

Although the shop's primary focus is flowers, there are some interesting containers and other gifts here. Jon and his associates make their own baskets from all kinds of indigenous materials, from willow to reeds to bittersweet. Popular wreaths are made from herbs or, for a southwestern twist, from succulents and cactus. Terra-cotta, ceramic and glass containers are a mainstay of the inventory.

Minimum: $35.00 plus delivery
All major credit cards
Also serves: Cerrillos, Eldorado, Espanola and Galisteo

NEW YORK

ALBANY

Glorious Blooms
Doug Stroup

298 Hudson Avenue
Albany, NY 12210
(518) 463-5531

Doug began his design career in graphics but soon found that flowers were the best medium in which to express his instinct to "create beautiful things." His goal is to have a diverse and constant selection of fresh and interesting flowers, "in order to get Albany beyond the carnation and 'mum' mode," he says. "My challenge here is to get people to develop the habit of buying flowers the way they now buy wine and cheese."

Although he imports flowers from all over the world, Doug also takes advantage of local horticultural talent. "Finally, local gardeners are coming to me with their seasonal perennials, herbs, flowering branches, annuals and little bits of all kinds of things. Their efforts give my inventory depth."

Although Doug and his associates are asked to do a myriad of design styles, he mostly creates loose, garden arrangements, usually in clear glass containers or baskets. The focus here is on flowers, so there's very little gift or accessory inventory. Creative holiday gifts are available—from boxwood trees decorated with flowers and attractive ornaments for Christmas, to Della Robbia topiaries for Thanksgiving.

Minimum: $25.00 plus delivery
All major credit cards
Also serves: Delmar, Colonie, Loudonville and Slingerlands

BRIDGEHAMPTON

Bridgehampton Florist
MICHAEL GRIMM

P.O. Box 1283
Main Street
Bridgehampton, NY 11932
(516) 537-7766

Many local gardeners keep Michael's shop well stocked with seasonal flowers and flowering plants. "We never keep a flower for more than two or three days. We'd rather give a bunch away to charities and high schools, because our customers have come to rely on our flowers being very fresh," says Michael. He imports flowers as well, and has tropicals on occasion.

For newborn babies Michael likes to send Bunnybees (from the same people who brought us Cabbage Patch dolls) attached to a single-stem beaker containing a specimen flower, with a balloon tied to the Bunnybee's little hand. "That way," Michael observes, "both the mother and the child get something, and it's affordable." Equally thoughtful and creative ideas are developed for other occasions as well.

Minimum: $25.00 plus delivery
All major credit cards
Also serves: East Hampton, Sag Harbor and Southampton

BUFFALO

Designs
DAN LOWRIE

311 Bryant Street
Buffalo, NY 14222
(716) 886-1669

When Dan opened his shop five years ago, his goal was to give clients an alternative to the predictable posies in baskets that most other florists were offering. Dan's style is unique. His creations often feature exotic tropical blooms in simple, uncluttered arrangements designed to show off each individual flower.

Individuality is a key word for Dan. "Each job is different," he says. "You listen to your clients, really take in what they say, and get a feeling about them. Then an idea for an arrangement they'd like just clicks."

Dan has been called the florist who has succeeded in bringing a New York City flavor to Buffalo. Traditional arrangements are available; but for those who want something a little different, a little more sophisticated, this is the place to go.

Minimum: $25.00 plus delivery
All major credit cards
Also serves: Amherst, Clarence, Cheektowaga, East Aurora, Hamburg, Grand Island, Lackawanna, Niagara Falls, Orchard Park, West Seneca and Williamsburg

Floristry
FANN MARKEL

1385 Delaware Avenue
Buffalo, NY 14209
(716) 885-6037

It's always amusing to hear how and why somebody goes into the floristry business, but I think Fann's story is the most ironic. She explains, "I started out as a painter and a golfer. That's my training. And as a hobby I often did my friends' flowers for their parties. I found I was spending more and more of my time arranging flowers and planning weddings and parties. It occurred to me that if I started a business, probably no one would call me."

Today, three thousand centerpieces later, not to mention a warehouse full of props, English antiques and urns, Fann's talents are dedicated to floristry. Her look is inspired by the English garden, giving her arrangements a sophisticated, well-trained charm. She also carries many proprietary gourmet food items.

When asked if she missed her painting, Fann replied, "Oh, we do that also. We do renderings for our weddings parties and trade shows. I hardly ever work from magazine pictures."

Minimum: $25.00 plus delivery
All major credit cards
Also serves: Amherst, Clarence, Cheektowaga, East Aurora, Grand Island, Hamburg, Lackawanna, Niagara Falls, Orchard Park, West Seneca and Williamsburg

CHAPPAQUA

Flowers By Frank Laning
FRANK LANING AIFD, AAF, PFCI

400 King Street
Chappaqua, NY 10414
(914) 238-5100

Frank describes his work as opulent and traditional. "It's old-fashioned, natural and unconstructed." Many local growers keep him supplied with seasonal garden flowers to combine with those he imports from all over the world. His goal is to embellish a given interior and never to do an arrangement that's at odds with the inherent feeling of a room.

Frank wants others to love and enjoy flowers as much as he does. For two hours every week he has his "flower market," when all the flowers, fresh daily, are marked down 50 percent in an effort to entice people who are unused to flowers.

Frank is such a legendary talent that he has been asked to direct the opening of American design schools in Japan. We're fortunate to have somebody with such style and such a wonderful personality to set the American standard in Japan. In addition, Frank teaches floral design at the New York Botanical Garden. As coordinator of the program, he has influenced many new designers.

Minimum: $30.00 plus delivery
All major credit cards
Also serves: Armonk, Bedford, Briarcliff Manor, Mount Kisco, Pleasantville and White Plains

FIRE ISLAND

Pistils and Peat
DON SUSSMAN AND MIKE FROHLICH

Bay Walk
Ocean Beach, NY 11770
(516) 583-5677

Since its opening day in 1976, Pistils and Peat has been the talk of Fire Island. Don and Mike's flowers, ranging from local snapdragons to Dutch lilies to Hawaiian heliconias arrive fresh off the boat four times a week in season. Colorful bouquets are wagoned, bicycled or water-taxied to all ends of the island. The owners and their staff personally know the majority of the island's summer and winter residents and will be glad to suggest appropriate gifts for someone's house, deck or garden. The house specialty is a beach wedding with all the trimmings—it's what dreams are made of.

Flowers may be arranged in a wide assortment of vases, baskets and pots, even in a wooden half-barrel. Try sending that through a wire service!

Minimum: $25.00 plus delivery
Credit to be arranged

LOCUST VALLEY

Little Flower House
KATE FLAMMIA

20 Oyster Bay Road
Locust Valley, NY 11560
(516) 671-8742

Mrs. Flammia is truly a flower lover. She grows almost everything she uses, and only when it is absolutely necessary does she order from Holland or California. Consequently, everything is always "in season," unless she's forced a bloom—of paper-white narcissus, crocus or azalea, for example—in one of her greenhouses. There's always something special here. Her arrangements are lovely; and with little direction, Mrs. Flammia tastefully executes any order.

"What I like to know from my customers are color choices and where they want to put it," she says, "so I can create the appropriate arrangement." She's one of the few people who can arrange gladiolus and make them look like they came from the garden and not the funeral parlor.

Minimum: $25.00; delivery charge only on orders to Manhattan
Credit card: American Express

MILLBROOK

Felicity Banford
FELICITY BANFORD

Woodstock Road
R.R. 3, Box 470
Millbrook, NY 13545
(914) 677-5640

Felicity hails from England, and in typical English fashion has been arranging flowers since she was a little girl. Her well-developed eye plus all that practice add up to a phenomenal talent. Her horticultural and design expertise extends to designing perennial borders and herb gardens, which adds real depth to her relationship with flowers. Natural garden bouquets ranging from a casual country look to grand and important compositions evoke emotional memories of beautiful summer days.

Felicity hand-selects flowers from the New York market as well as culling seasonal herbs and perennials from her own garden.

Daily arrangements are created in handsome baskets, terra-cotta pots or clear glass vases. Her sophisticated use of dried flowers and other materials that she has prepared herself results in topiaries and arrangements that are a cut above the usual.

Minimum: $35.00 plus delivery
3 days' notice, but Felicity prefers a week
Best at market
Credit to be arranged
Also serves: In New York: Amenia, Poughkeepsie and Rhinebeck; in Connecticut: Sharon

JWF Horticulture
JOHN W. FALLS

The Goose Chase
P.O. Box 4
Millbrook, NY 12545
(518) 398-6676

Although John arranges lovely bouquets for parties and local extravaganzas, for long-distance service he limits his creations to fabulous wooden flats or terra-cotta pots of seasonal bulbs: hyacinths, tulips, crocuses, daffodils, lilies of all kinds, from callas to Casablancas, and assorted perennials in bloom. The list is more extensive, just ask what he's got. You can also choose between having the bulbs planted with grass or simply by themselves. This sort of gift is perfect for the sophisticated though practical tastes of Millbrook, one of the most beautiful places in the country.

Minimum: $40.00 plus delivery
24-hour notice required
Credit to be arranged
Also serves: Amenia and Rhinebeck

NEW YORK CITY

Les Fleurs de Maxim's
PIERRE CARDIN; OLIVIER GUINI, DIRECTOR
680 Madison Avenue
New York, NY 10021
(212) 752-9889

In 1980 Pierre Cardin started Les Fleurs de Maxim's in Paris with Olivier Guini. When Mr. Cardin decided to open a shop in New York City last year in conjunction with Maxim's restaurant, he asked Olivier to start the operation. Fortunately for us, Olivier loves New York and has decided to stay.

He has a unique style that finds its roots in the Belle Epoque. In keeping with that time, his arrangements have an art nouveau feeling, which is consistent with the decor in Maxim's. The style takes off from a concept that Cardin pioneered, based on the use of dominant leaves that highlight and provide a setting for the flowers. Indeed, flowers are somewhat secondary to the exotic or tropical foliage. Large leaves such as *Anthericum cristalinum*, monstera or apes or finely textured bamboo or bear grass is used as a prop for the flowers' colors, which peek around the edges or float up from the base of the leaves. It's boldly architectural, and handsome.

Olivier arranges the flowers and foliage in a vase almost effortlessly, avoiding the manipulations that some English and Japanese arrangers impose on their materials. I doubt many others could pull it off, but Olivier can. And like many really great designers, he didn't learn it in school, but does it by instinct.

Flowers are sold only in vases or as bouquets. The bouquets are not just loose flowers; they are arranged and need only to be set into a vase. If you do order a container from Les Fleurs de Maxim's, it will be either a column or a vase made exclusively for the shop based on Cardin's private collection in Paris. There is an abundance of enthusiasm here, and understandably so—the work is unique.

Minimum: $50.00 plus delivery
All major credit cards

Helena Lehane
HELENA LEHANE

116 East 62nd Street
New York, NY 10021
(212) 888-7763

Voluptuous and energetic combinations of important flowers in dozens of soft colors set Helena's Rubenesque arrangements apart from the usual variety you see at many of New York's finest florists. With sincere humility, Helena is often amazed by her work, as though she can't believe she actually put together the arrangement. "There's no question my fingers are blessed with divine magic," she says. "Every day I thank God for my talent."

With confidence and discretion she respectfully arranges for the crème de la crème of New York society. Consultations in her studio are by appointment only. We're fortunate to have her in *Fine Flowers by Phone.*

Minimum: $100.00 plus delivery
24-hour notice required
Credit to be arranged

Mädderlake
ALAN BOEHMER, BILLY JARECKI AND TOM PRITCHARD

25 East 73rd Street (at Madison Avenue)
New York, NY 10021
(212) 879-8400

Many people are familiar with the designers at Mädderlake from their *Flowers Rediscovered: New Ideas for Using and Enjoying Flowers* (New York: Stewart, Tabori

& Chang, 1985), a carefully reasoned and beautifully illustrated volume. The Mädderlake designers prefer to showcase the natural beauty of the flowers in their arrangements rather than the art of the arranger. Their work has an elegant simplicity spiced with a dash of casual abandon. Their style, a careful combination of country charm and urban sophistication, is exciting and new.

Mädderlake's flowers come from a wide variety of sources, from locally grown perennials, berried branches and forced flowering branches to the best of Holland, Israel and the south of France. Out of season their local sources provide extravagant boxes of tulips of all sorts, baskets of lilies of the valley and trays of miniature bulbs, from checkerboard lilies to the tiniest of daffodils. During the warmer seasons there is an endless supply of uncommon garden flowers.

Believing that an offering of flowers is an expression of love and caring, the people at Mädderlake take great care in their work, from the initial moment of choice all the way through to the way the flowers are wrapped, ribboned and delivered. Just state your budget, and leave the rest to them. Your order is in some of this country's most talented and tasteful hands.

Minimum: $60.00 plus delivery
All major credit cards

Ronaldo Maia
RONALDO MAIA

57 East 67th Street
New York, NY 10021
(212) 288-1049

An aesthetic change affecting flower arranging has been occurring over the past fifteen years, but not at the same rate everywhere. Bit by bit we started seeing flowers displayed individually in clear bud vases, scattered on dining-room tables or grouped on chests and coffee tables. The traditional florists' "roundy moundy" was giving way to a new, more natural vitality.

In the early seventies new materials, such as raffia, gray moss and curly willow began to be used. The genesis of this innovation in flower design took place in Ronaldo Maia's workshop and studio in New York City, a development beautifully documented in Denise Otis and Ronaldo Maia's *Decorating with Flowers* (New York: Harry N. Abrams, 1978), a must in every flower lover's library.

Ronaldo, as talented now as ever, is constantly developing exciting gift ideas. And expensive as it is, a creation by this artist is well worth the price. His standard dried-moss topiary tree gracefully decorated with dried rose buds anchored in a neoclassic-inspired terra-cotta pot is a standout in its genre. These trees work wonderfully in almost any setting. Ronaldo's blends of scented potpourri are famous and harmonize subtly with his line of scented candles. All gift items here are au courant, and tasteful.

If you are in New York, a trip to Ronaldo Maia, just off Madison Avenue, is worth every minute.

Minimum: $45.00 plus delivery
Credit card: American Express

Renny
RENNY REYNOLDS

159 East 64th Street
New York, NY 10021
(212) 288-7000

Renny Reynolds is best known as a party designer, and it's easy to see why. Descriptions of his parties are memorable. For one he lined a long entrance with classically designed columns topped with huge blocks of dry ice and, above that, wonderfully exotic arrangements lighted from the inside. Guests were enveloped by clouds of dramatic "smoke" as they arrived for the party. Sensational!

Renny has made a name for himself with his retail shop as well. I recommend the potted bulbs and orchids here, along with one of his wonderful containers.

Minimum: $35.00 plus delivery
All major credit cards

Salou
PAT BRAUN AND STEVE LILIE

452A Columbus Avenue
New York, NY 10024
(212) 595-9604

Salou is the art of flower arranging at its zenith. From this shop's designers you can always expect restrained opulence in their grand and sophisticated combinations of imported Dutch and garden flowers. Pat Braun, a former partner at Mädderlake, contributed to the creative genius of that shop.

Salou offers a brochure highlighting dozens of thoughtful gift ideas. To a friend in bed with the flu they will deliver a bouquet of flowers along with a bowl of homemade chicken soup. To a hospital patient will go a similar bouquet along with a selection of magazines. Sounds obvious, but not many other florists will do things like this.

Minimum: $50.00 plus delivery
All major credit cards

Twigs
PAUL BOTT

381 Bleecker Street
New York, NY 10014
(212) 620-8188

In a word, the look here is Victorian. And there's much more going on at Twigs than flower arranging. Great attention is paid to every detail. Beautiful French ribbons are carefully knotted around bouquets, and the designers choose from a constantly changing innovative selection of proprietary items. Last Valentine's Day, for example, Paul commissioned three sizes of flowered chintz hatboxes, in which he placed appropriate-sized nosegays. It made a romantic and different gift. So be sure to ask what's new.

You can often see Twigs's work in *House Beautiful* and *Bride* magazines.

Minimum: $35.00 plus delivery
All major credit cards

VSF
SPRUCE RODEN AND JACK FOLLMER

204 West Tenth Street
New York, NY 10014
(212) 206-7236

Spruce and Jack find their inspiration in eighteenth-century design. Their work is restrained, intelligent, rarefied, and unpretentious. The soft palette of loosely mixed foliage and flowers in grays and greens, pinks, whites and lavenders takes the hard edge off an otherwise austere discipline. Yet they're also not afraid to use strong colors if the occasion calls for it.

They carry a good selection of topiaries, but not the ordinary ivies and boxwoods. Instead, they have curious flowering plants and herbs made up into trees, tiers and shapes. They also display special gift items. They carry wonderful flowerpots that are gold leafed, oxidized or given interesting *faux* finishes. Their intricately woven swags and garlands of muted dried materials are appropriate for almost any setting.

As in eighteenth-century design, every detail is considered an opportunity for aesthetic possibilities. For orchids, Spruce and Jack use a silver-plated wire stake, oxidized and shaped to mimic the curve of the orchid bloom while simultaneously lending support. For their tiny, perfect dried topiary trees they often substitute the expected twig branch with a surprising braided brass trunk.

These are very special flowers.

Minimum: $50.00 plus delivery
Credit card: American Express

ZeZe
ZEZE

398 East 52nd Street
New York, NY 10022
(212) 753-7767

Elegant but simple is the way ZeZe describes his work. But even with the simplest of arrangements he achieves a charming romanticism. Flowers that change according to season will be mixed with herbs in the summer or variegated ivy in winter.

"I never box my flowers," he says. "Boxes hide the flowers." Instead, he uses cellophane tied with ribbons in three colors. And every potted plant or orchid is transplanted into terra-cotta. There is also a line of specially designed vases, and at holiday times you'll find a number of unique gift items, such as the handmade wreaths for Valentine's Day.

ZeZe's work has been featured in *The New York Times Magazine* and *Town and Country*.

Minimum: $40.00 plus delivery
Credit card: American Express

NORTH SALEM

Grand Designs
CECILY GRAND

RFD 2, Hawley Road
North Salem, NY 10560
(914) 669-8270

When Cecily Grand moved here from San Francisco seven years ago, she decided to make the transition from shop owner to free-lancer.

She's always coming up with sensible and adorable ideas. In the fall, for example, a carved pumpkin serves as the base for a flower arrangement. The carving is done in such a way that the arrangement sits on the top while the light from the candle inside the jack-o'-lantern still shines through. Whatever "Grand" twist she creates, Cecily's natural arrangements combine lots of Holland imports and natives in lovely, loose bouquets.

Minimum: $45.00 plus delivery
Credit to be arranged

OLD CHATHAM

Claudia Kingsley
CLAUDIA KINGSLEY

Route 66
Malden Bridge, NY 12115
(518) 766-4759

Claudia combines her floral talents with an eye for inexpensive country antiques. "I don't carry a lot of investment antiques; these are things you can use, and I use many of them with flowers, from cut glass and colored pottery to pine boxes and baskets."

Specify how much you want to spend, and then just ask Claudia for a suggestion. Whatever you decide on, her country arrangements can stand up on their own, shouting with dramatic flair.

Minimum: $30.00 plus delivery
Credit cards: MasterCard and VISA

POUND RIDGE

L. H. Greene
LARRY GREENE

RR3 Box 10A, Westchester Avenue
Pound Ridge, NY 10576
(914) 764-4006

With great skill Larry and his designers achieve that perfect balance between homemade simplicity and urban sophistication. Their work is something like a Noland painting—it looks as if you could do it yourself, but you can't. Larry personally chooses all his flowers at market and combines them in an elegantly simple, loose way.

L. H. Greene is reminiscent of a shop in the old Covent Garden. It's tiny—only seven hundred square feet—and filled with gorgeous containers, some made specially in lead, glass and terra-cotta. Larry has antique terra-cotta containers, too, in unusual shapes. He's the only florist I've spoken to who sometimes even makes his own baskets. These require a few days' notice, of course. At L. H. Greene, you'll find loads of topiaries, unusual plants, orchids and a lot of style.

Minimum: $45.00 plus delivery
Credit cards: MasterCard and VISA
Also serves: Bedford, Katonah and South Salem; in Connecticut: Darien, Canaan and Stamford

ROCHESTER

Arena Florists
CHUCK ARENA

260 East Avenue
Rochester, NY 14604
(716) 454-3720

All the activity in this shop, set in a refurbished brick warehouse in Rochester's inner loop, revolves around an attractive kiosk that displays the sixty or so varieties of cut flowers available on a daily basis. It is the focal point of the store, set in the middle of the studiolike space where designers and customers make their personal selection of flowers. Most are imported from all over the world, but many are locally grown seasonal perennials, annuals and herbs.

This colorful display inspires Chuck and his associates to create arrangements that span the aesthetic spectrum. "We have a lot of looks going on here," says Chuck. "We're known for our contemporary, high-style look that is softened by an instinctual respect for the natural rhythm of the materials. We don't manipulate the life out of our flowers." Loose mixed bouquets are also part of the daily agenda. Be sure to let the designer know your preferences.

There is an exciting choice of blooming plants, from orchids to bromeliads, as well as a diverse selection of containers—clear glass vases, baskets and ceramics. Loose flowers are presented in one of two ways: wrapped in clear cellophane and tied with a white cloth ribbon with the shop name inscribed in black print, or placed in a glossy black box filled with black opalescent tissue and tied with silver or gold lamé ribbon.

Minimum: $30.00 plus delivery
All major credit cards
Also serves: Brighton, Brockport, Bushnelle's Basin, Canandaigua, Chili, Churchville, Fairport, Gates, Greece, Henrietta, Hilton, Honeoye Falls, Irondequoit, Mendon, Penfield, Perinton, Scottsville, Spencerport and Victor

SARATOGA SPRINGS

Dehn's Flowers
CHARLES DEHN

178 Beekman Street
Saratoga Springs, NY 12866
(518) 584-1880

Two city blocks of greenhouses
and workrooms trot to the tune of the racetrack here. Dehn's has
been around since 1892, and without a doubt, Charles Dehn knows
his customers. He knows everybody's racing colors, and that usually dictates the flower arrangements, unless it's the customer who
likes only white flowers.

Dehn's supplies the town, as well as the racetrack, with all
the bedding plants it needs. My advice here is to state what you
want, whether it's a loose bouquet or a dozen rubrum lilies, and
keep it simple.

Minimum: $15.00 plus delivery
All major credit cards
Also serves: Ballston Spa, Corinth, Greenwich and Schuylerville

SCARSDALE

Colonial Village Flowers
JOE WARD

1515 Weaver Street
Scarsdale, NY 10583
(914) 723-2888

"Joe's an artist. He knows what an
arrangement is going to look like before he starts," says an enthusi-

astic associate. More important to us, he loves flowers and is an avid horticulturist—he's constantly growing things for the shop in his greenhouse, from sweet peas to flowering kale. Other flowers are handpicked at market.

Joe's talents span the floral spectrum, from contemporary to English-garden inspirations. On many occasions, however, he sneaks in a restrained flair. One of his old-time favorites is an oblong flat basket, the bottom of which is covered in moss or baby's tears, with a cluster of one kind of flower massed straight into the base. "It looks like a chunk of the garden." Miniature images evoking memories of large vistas! Divine.

Minimum: $30.00 plus delivery
All major credit cards
Also serves: Surrounding suburbs

The Greenery Florist
ELIZABETH WOLFF

205 East Hartsdale Avenue
Hartsdale, NY 10530
(914) 472-0922

As the name implies, there is a wealth of greenery here: plants, orchids and other blooming specimens. For cut flowers, arrangements are typically "elegant English to country English" in baskets of all colors, but more often natural or whitewashed ones. Contemporary arrangements are created in low, black Lomey water dishes—anthuriums, for example, are combined off center in the dish with bear grass, and Oriental designs are created with bamboo and orchids. "As if you were looking into a water garden," is how Elizabeth Wolff describes these arrangements.

Ms. Wolff is impressively knowledgeable in horticulture and has been closely connected with the New York Botanical Garden, as teacher and lecturer, for twenty years. This intense dedication to the world of flowers and foliage has given her an immense and uninhibited awareness of materials that can be used decoratively, as her window displays always demonstrate.

Be specific with your order.

Minimum: $25.00 plus delivery
All major credit cards
Also serves: Bronxville, Elmsford, Hartsdale, Purchase, Scarsdale and White Plains

SOUTHAMPTON

Artistry in Flowers
PHILIP BIANCO

27 Hampton Road
Southampton, NY 11968
(516) 283-8200

A splendid assortment of flowering plants, perennials, garden flowers, tropicals and topiaries presents Philip Bianco's customers with a delightfully difficult choice. And when Philip himself gets involved, the decisions become even more complex, because he's always presenting new and daring combinations as well as more traditional suggestions. For example, he plants cerise bougainvillea, red geraniums and pink hibiscus all in the same rolled Italian terra-cotta pot for the porch, creating a riot of color, perfect for a beach house—very Caribbean! Or he can do a simple yet stately grouping of tall, narrow glass vases with a specimen bloom in each one for a cool but dramatic display appropriate for just about anywhere.

As you can imagine, to serve successfully the well-heeled and demanding clientele of Southampton, one must have a special talent. Philip does, so you can leave the details to him. Rest assured he creates all things beautiful.

Minimum: $35.00 plus delivery
All major credit cards

Also serves: Bridgehampton, East Hampton, Hampton Bays, Sagaponack, Sag Harbor, Wainscott, Water Mill and Westhampton Beach

SYRACUSE

Five Seasons
DAN McCANN

7076 Cedar Bay Road
Fayetteville, NY 13066
(315) 446-3275

Whether it's a picnic, a party or a bedroom bouquet, Dan's goal is to set the mood and capture the moment. "So people remember it," he says. "And I do this without being intrusive." Dan has a special knack that enables him to know what people want and a tasteful touch that imbues any setting with a quiet magic.

Flowers are combined to enhance their natural beauty. A bunch of hops are gathered from the woods, casually combined with a few gardenias, or handsome bittersweet baskets are filled with pale pink tulips. Nothing is studied; everything is custom. "This is a small town, and my clients don't want repetition; however, I respect their specific tastes, whether it's gardenias to fill a silver cigarette box or vases of blue iris."

Dan has kept his inventory varied by developing relationships with nearby Canadians, who supply him with an abundance of native materials. A greenhouse connected to the shop is filled with foliage and blooming plants and a terrific selection of orchids.

Minimum: $25.00 plus delivery
Credit cards: MasterCard and VISA
Also serves: Fayetteville and surrounding suburbs

NORTH CAROLINA

ASHEVILLE

Celebration
GAIL MARTIN

207 Charlotte Street
Asheville, NC 28801
(704) 253-1789

Bouquets from Celebration range from pretty, soft arrangements to a sophisticated wildflower look. Flowers from all over the world are combined with locally grown perennials and herbs such as yarrow, feverfew, cornflowers, garden roses or sunflowers. Gail scans the woods and hillsides for seasonally blooming branches as well as for native grasses and foliages like magnolias and rhododendrons. Assorted blooming plants and orchids are also available.

Attractive gift ideas exemplify Gail's restrained sensibility: handsome baskets filled with armfuls of cut lavender flowers; Christmas centerpieces in mixed shades of foliage that create a seasonal harmony. Arrangements go out in clear glass vases, terracotta pots or baskets.

The shop is filled with antiques—both furniture and decorative accessories—in a range of styles from Queen Anne to French to painted Hepplewhite.

Minimum: **$35.00 plus delivery**
Credit cards: MasterCard and VISA
Also serves: **Arden, Skyland and Swannanoa**

Clement's Flower Shop
FRED LEMMONDS AND JOHN E. GROOMS

462 Sweeten Creek Road
Asheville, NC 28803
(704) 274-2140

In small towns far from the hub
of metropolitan areas, it makes sense that a dependable florist has
a greenhouse operation extensive enough to cater to discriminating
tastes. Such is the case with Clement's. The proprietors grow what
they sell and, when appropriate, combine their own flora with
imports, creating airy, casual arrangements. They also do daring
and dramatic contemporary arrangements.

Be sure to be specific about what you do and don't want.

Minimum: $30.00 plus delivery
All major credit cards
Also serves: Arden, Skyland and Swannanoa

CHARLOTTE

The Blossom Shop
DEBORAH SACRA AND TED TODD

2242 Park Road
Charlotte, NC 28203
(704) 376-3526

In business since 1929, The
Blossom Shop has developed a reputation as a trendsetter, giving
Charlotte the best the floral industry has to offer in products and
design. Presentations range from glitzy contemporary to traditional

European garden mixtures. They have a wide variety of cut flowers, locally grown and imported. Extensive greenhouses are filled with tropical foliage, blooming plants, bromeliads and up to six varieties of orchids. A landscaping department specializing in borders, herb gardens and even Oriental gardens lends depth to the proprietors' appreciation of the natural integrity of flowers.

Many clients comment on the professional ease with which the shop handles large functions, both personal and corporate. It is so well known for this that Deborah and Ted are often asked to travel to other cities and states. They have been able to provide unique arrangements and personal service as well as designs for large functions by creating a working environment for their associates that fosters learning.

The Blossom Shop combines southern charm with a contemporary approach and Old World craftsmanship, making this a traditional favorite in Charlotte. Nonetheless, keep your order specific and detailed.

Minimum: $25.00 plus delivery
All major credit cards
Also serves: Matthews, Mint Hill and Pineville

Curt Christiansen Florist
CURT CHRISTIANSEN

214 Providence Road
Charlotte, NC 28207
(704) 377-2210

I t's clear that Curt's on the ball. He works on a reciprocal basis with designers from shops all over the country, in a kind of floral exchange program.

Curt carries a large inventory of specialty linens and tablecloths and other party necessities, which can be rented wherever you may need them. He also carries a carefully chosen collection of proprietary products, including designs by Englishman Kenneth Turner, which he culls from the stock of other florists.

His floral style spans the spectrum from traditional to modern. Whatever you order, it will be eclectic and imbued with enthusiasm. "There's nothing new in this world," says Mr. Christiansen. "You just have to learn how to adapt it to the time or trend." Given just a few descriptive generalizations, Curt's more than capable of taking care of the details with integrity and talent.

Minimum: $20.00 plus delivery
Credit to be arranged
Also serves: Matthews, Mint Hill and Pineville

Fresh Innovations
PAT MCCALL

1808 East Independence Boulevard
Charlotte, NC 28205
(704) 335-0095

For many years Pat McCall's work has brought flair and imagination to the Charlotte area, and for a long time her clients considered her the best-kept secret in town. She describes her work as innovative and natural, with a European look—loose and airy, but textured. I agree, but to complete the picture I must add that her arrangements are always in good taste.

Pat works on her own; she doesn't employ any other designers. She combines flowers grown specially for her and those from her own garden with imports: roses, seasonal perennials, herbs and annuals. And she has cutting privileges for greenery and branches at local gardens. She doesn't carry any foliage plants, though she will special-order seasonal blooming plants and bulbs and orchids. A big choice of material combined with Pat's talents adds up to fabulous fountains of flowers, abundantly planted European baskets or beautifully arranged plants in terra-cotta trays.

Minimum: $35.00 plus delivery
24-hour notice required
Credit to be arranged

DURHAM

Flowers
SALLY LANTZ

Brightleaf Square
Main Street
Durham, NC 27701
(919) 688-2855

Sally got started in the flower business for a reason analogous to mine for beginning this book; she had grown weary of not having quality flowers and arrangements in her town, just as I had become exasperated trying to send fine flowers long-distance. She's now dedicated to supplying this quality in Durham.

Sally's shop is strictly devoted to flowers. It's not unusual for her to have eighty different kinds of flowers there on any one day—from Dutch and French imports to all kinds of tropicals from Hawaii and New Zealand, as well as wildflowers from California. She does not carry houseplants or flowering plants and does not do traditional funeral work. Flowers is a specialized shop dedicated to cut flowers and party work.

Sally describes her work as "loose and airy with pizzazz." Lots of berries, fruits and vegetables will be artfully incorporated into her arrangements, and she is intent on carrying a large selection of unusual greens: silver-dollar yuke or kochia, boxwood and variegated pittosporum.

There is also a huge inventory of tablecloths, all exquisite, for rental anywhere—so if you need green moiré with lace overlays or a chintz tablecloth, just call. And you can find a selection of containers and accessories for the house or garden. Be sure to ask about the many special holiday ideas. But remember, the emphasis here is on the flowers, and they are exquisite, both individually and in arrangements.

Minimum: $25.00 plus delivery
All major credit cards
Also serves: Chapel Hill

RALEIGH

Carlton
CARLTON LONG

527 Hillsborough Street
Raleigh, NC 27603
(919) 821-3862

At a busy cross section in downtown Raleigh any passerby is pleasantly startled by the magical scenes Carlton displays in his windows. Last Christmas two-dimensional silver and gold Christmas trees were lighted by thousands of little bulbs, iridescent icicles hung from the ceiling, and "snow" drifted everywhere, creating a winter wonderland.

His arrangements take on the same explosion of energy, perhaps due to the dramatic use of space between the flowers. Tropicals or Dutch flowers are designed in low trays, terra-cotta containers or ceramic vases. "We do very little in baskets," he notes. It's a sophisticated, clean look.

Minimum: $30.00 plus delivery
All major credit cards
Also serves: Cary, Garner, Knightdale and Research Triangle Park

WINSTON-SALEM

Price Davis Florist
PRICE DAVIS

1214 Reynolda Road
Winston-Salem, NC 27104
(919) 724-2270

Although sometimes confined by traditional expectations, Price is steadfastly and courageously taking the aesthetic leap into the new world of floral design that this book is all about. It's a transition that few floral shops want to make, much less can successfully accomplish. Yet Price is succeeding. Congratulations! Just let him know exactly what you want.

Minimum: $25.00 plus delivery
All major credit cards

OHIO

AKRON

Architectural Greenery
CECELIA J. ("C.J.") AND JOHN R. BAKER

1028 Jefferson Avenue
Akron, OH 44302
(216) 867-4421

Flowers from C.J. always command immediate attention and plenty of rave notices for their spectacular appeal. Perhaps the main reason for this is the special effort given to putting unusual and exotic flowers together with accents of perfect greens. Depending on the season, lilies, proteas, orchids or tulips are combined with architectural greens from her large inventory of tropical plants or from her own garden.

"My approach to floral design is extremely personal in that each design has unique appeal for the occasion intended. To achieve this, I spend adequate time with each client, eliciting his or her exact needs," C.J. explains. Her design expertise favors the loose and airy, with each flower proclaiming its individuality.

The shop is also filled with many specimen plants for sale or rent.

Minimum: $25.00 plus delivery
Credit cards: MasterCard and VISA
Also serves: Canton

CINCINNATI

The Dennis Buttelwerth Florist
DENNIS BUTTELWERTH

3438 Edwards Road
Cincinnati, OH 45208
(513) 321-3611

Dennis is the kind of florist many people seek. His talents are traditional, and his standards for quality and professionalism are high. His work had become so popular at one point that he finally rewrote the rules, limiting his services. "I was killing myself," he remarked. Now he does only one function a day in addition to everyday business. And what's refreshing is that he doesn't care whether it's a gala ball or a hundred-dollar wedding. Dennis is a person who truly gives of himself.

His work mimics his eclectic personality. Arrangements span the spectrum, from extremely high style to English-garden bouquets. Nothing is country, however. Garden flowers are grown especially for the shop: veronica, zinnias, seven types of yarrow and

Balloon flowers (platycodon), to name a few. Otherwise they are imported directly.

Dennis is innovative as well. Potpourri covers the mechanics in an arrangement as often as moss does. He says, "I never do anything twice, but people can always tell when I have done the work." His shop is filled with porcelains and crystals, Chinese export ware and baskets, some of which are woven with leather.

Minimum: $35.00 plus delivery
All major credit cards

CLEVELAND

D. K. Vanderbrook Florist, Inc.
DONALD K. VANDERBROOK

3113 Mayfield Road (at Lee)
Cleveland Heights, OH 44118
(216) 371-0164

A quarter of a century after starting as a simple florist shop, D. K. Vanderbrook has evolved into a full-service business that requires Donald Vanderbrook and his design team to travel back and forth between coasts. Memorable to many of us from photographs and television coverage are the spectacular rose displays created for Prince Charles and Princess Diana during their stay at the British Embassy in Washington, DC.

Mr. Vanderbrook is also well known as a rose hybridizer, and as an excellent gardener. He maintains four acres of formal English and wildflower gardens, and he has access to thirty acres of perennial flowers. While many of his flowers are specially grown for retail sales, the gardens are also a testing ground to determine the value of specific flowers for display and cutting.

Unquestionably, there is a great deal of depth here, as well as good taste. Mr. Vanderbrook has been influenced by Sheila Macqueen, with whom he studied.

Minimum: $45.00 plus delivery
All major credit cards

The Village Greenery
JUDY RAMLOW AND DAISY ("PETE") HUCKLICK

8173 Colombia
Cleveland, OH 44138
(216) 235-5011

Work at The Village Greenery can be far-out and avant-garde or of the more traditional, garden-arrangement type, but with a twist. Hydrangeas, lisianthus and rubrum lilies are interspersed with tall swatches of grasses.

Occasionally Judy and Pete like to include an appropriate gift with an arrangement. "We'll incorporate a peacock fan into a hospital arrangement and sign the card "From your fan club." For children we use Beatrix Potter animals and books in little landscapes." Whatever Judy and Pete are doing, their mission is to add a touch of personal artistry to their arrangements. The Village Greenery provides both the floral expertise and the sensitivity to assist the customer, who should be specific about his or her requirements.

Minimum: $30.00 plus delivery
All major credit cards

DAYTON

PETALS Cut Flowers & Bouquets
JOYCE CLEMENS

719 Shroyer Road
Dayton, OH 45419
(513) 293-6419

When Joyce opened PETALS, her original intention was to run only a cut-flower market. "I was frustrated by the lack of a source for pretty flowers in this town," she remembers. As time passed, customers began asking her to do parties and weddings, and eventually the demand for her floral talents turned her market into a full-service florist.

Joyce's fine-arts background found expression through her flowers; her style is predominantly English flowers arranged in a loose and natural way. Imported flowers are combined with seasonally available meadow flowers such as ironweed, Queen Anne's lace, black-eyed Susan and wild carrot.

The shop, heralded by an award-winning logo on the front window, is filled with fresh and dried flowers and a variety of baskets and clear glass containers. Only during holidays is there an abundant supply of blooming plants; otherwise, all Joyce's energies are focused on cut flowers. The results are spectacular!

Minimum: $25.00 plus delivery
Credit cards: MasterCard and VISA

TOLEDO

Keith Brooks
KEITH BROOKS

5577 Monroe Street
Sylvania, OH 43560
(419) 882-1106

This handbook could hardly have been written much more than three years ago, because the new trend in floristry had not yet spread to even the largest cities. Toledo is a case in point. It wasn't until three years ago that the wholesalers here began supplying the city's retail shops with Holland flowers on a regular basis, and florists like Keith Brooks were the ones who had a lot to do with them changing their ways. No doubt Mr. Brooks has catered to Toledo's carriage trade for some time, or he wouldn't have had the clout to help convince the wholesalers to carry new merchandise.

As in many towns, the taste in flowers here runs the gamut from high-style contemporary arrangements that feature a specimen bloom to large, loose bouquets in wonderful baskets. Whatever the style, Keith firmly believes that flowers shouldn't be jammed into a vase. He says, "Stems can be as important as the flowers themselves."

Minimum: $30.00 plus delivery
All major credit cards
Also serves: Maumee, Perrysburg and Sylvania

OKLAHOMA

OKLAHOMA CITY

Trochta's
JIM VALLION

P.O. Box 14250
Oklahoma City, OK 73313
(405) 848-3338

J im is Oklahoma City's finest caterer, and six years ago he indulged his love of flowers when he bought Trochta's, the town's traditional florist. The operative description of his work is *value*. Jim's own greenhouses supply the shop with everything from hibiscus trees to orchids to chrysanthemums. Such vertical integration keeps costs—and prices—down.

The work here is comfortably appealing, not daring, but always in good taste.

Minimum: $30.00 plus delivery
All major credit cards
Also serves: Edmond

TULSA

Mary Murray's Flowers
MARY MURRAY

London Square
5800 South Lewis
Tulsa, OK 74105
(918) 743-6145

A profusion of delphiniums, fully-blown roses, liatris, gerberas, lilies and lilacs are always a part of Ms. Murray's work. After all, she considers herself a spring person, "and here we stretch spring over ten and a half months of the year; but we do bow to Christmas and Thanksgiving," she says. Loose, open and airy is the way she describes her work, yet "I always try to extract from customers just where the arrangement is going to go. No matter how good the arrangement is, if it isn't appropriate for the setting, then I have failed."

The selection of proprietary products here reveals the mark of a truly great designer. There are Italian silk flowers, poolside trash containers that hold blooming plants and, for baby gifts, a presentation arranged around a picture frame, with the child's name written in calligraphy on a piece of paper that is placed within the frame, where the picture will go.

No detail is overlooked. All gift cards are written in calligraphy with a specially blended ink in hunter green to match the color of the shop's logo. Ms. Murray says, "You know, people keep cards as mementos, and ours are very pretty." Too bad we can't keep one of her spectacular arrangements forever. They're breathtaking.

Minimum: $25.00 plus delivery
All major credit cards

OREGON

PORTLAND

Richard Calhoun Design Studio
RICHARD CALHOUN

403 NW Ninth Avenue
Portland, OR 97209
(503) 223-1646

"**S**lick but not contrived," is the way Richard describes his work. Arrangements are contemporary with an Oriental feel. The hard lines often inherent in this kind of work are softened by a gentle touch and the use of natural materials—no Lucite rods or copper tubing here. Although polished to a fine finish, it's graceful.

Local growers keep the studio supplied with seasonal favorites of Richard's: black tulips, parrot and French tulips, Cecile Brunner and other garden roses, quince and a wealth of perennials. He likes to use glass or highly glazed containers or his own bamboo ones. Just remember, Richard is prepared and able to do anything.

Minimum: $30.00 plus delivery
Credit cards: MasterCard and VISA
Also serves: Aloha, Beaverton, Charbonneau, Clackamas, Gresham, Lake Oswego, Milwaukie, Oregon City, Tigard and West Linn; in Washington: Vancouver

Dorcas Flowers
BOB CRAMER AND ALLEN SIMMONS

525 SW Broadway
Portland, OR 97205
(503) 227-6454

"Anything we like, we buy, and we sell, from Chinese export ware to Oriental rugs to Italian terracotta," says Mr. Cramer. Undoubtedly, he and Allen Simmons have a lot of fun.

While maintaining a natural approach to flowers, their energetic imaginations tackle every detail. Such flowers as Iceland poppies, tree peonies, alchemilla (lady's-mantle) and calla lilies are grown in a number of local gardens just for their shop. Others are shipped in from all over the world. Styles range from country French to very sophisticated. For Easter they've been known to deliver baskets of planted grass with live bunnies or chicks. But most important, their sensibility defers to subtlety. "We want our flowers to sit comfortably in any interior, not giving the impression of having been professionally manhandled, but as if our customers gathered them up from the garden and casually placed them in the container themselves," says Mr. Simmons. We all know it takes a lot of talent to achieve the impression of elegant simplicity.

Minimum: $25.00 plus delivery
Credit cards: MasterCard and VISA
Also serves: Aloha, Beaverton, Charbonneau, Gresham, Lake Oswego, Oregon City, Tigard and West Linn; in Washington: Vancouver

SALEM

Triple Tree Florists
JACK RICHARDS, AIFD, AND HERBERT PIEKOW

310 Court Street, NE
Salem, OR 97301
(503) 581-4226

Jack Richards has devoted his life to the world of flowers. Before becoming a partner at Triple Tree he was a landscape architect and had taught the Biedermeier style of flower arranging in Japan.

An impressive amount of the material Jack and Herbert use in their shop comes from their own gardens, where they gather armloads of seasonal flowering branches like lilac, and cut flowers such as delphinium, lilies and lavender. Their inventory includes numerous species of viburnum as well as azaleas, rhododendron, flowering fruit trees, floribunda roses, fragrant herbs and fresh annuals. They supplement their garden-grown flowers with bi-weekly shipments from all over the world.

Regarding their floral style, Jack states, "We are not locked into any one style. Our work ranges from a strong-line contemporary look to casual." Daily arrangements go out in your choice of either a clear glass container or a basket. Blooming plants and herbs are delicately mixed together in planted baskets or handsome strawberry crates. Assorted terra-cotta pots and topiary plants are also available. The shop is filled with an extensive gift line, all horticulturally related. There is a lot of choice and talent here; just be specific about what you want.

Minimum: $25.00 plus delivery
All major credit cards
Also serves: Keizer

PENNSYLVANIA

JOHNSTOWN

The Flower Barn
GEORGE A. GRIFFITH AND THOMAS J. O'BRIEN, AIFD

Millcreek Road at Buckness Avenue
P.O. Box 1
Johnstown, PA 15905/for mail: 15907
(814) 536-4431

The two talented horticulturists at The Flower Barn have not only developed an important national reputation that has led them all over the country to design parties and weddings, but they have also earned an unequaled reputation for their knowledge of aquatic plants. On their list of clients is the White House, where they have been invited to display water lilies and other aquatic plants for state dinners. Theirs is one of the largest commercial botanical plant collections in the northeast, with some fifty thousand square feet of greenhouse space, extensive nurseries and propagation areas. George and Thomas are unexcelled in their accomplishments in the hybridizing of aquatic plants.

Flowers are the tools they use to create an atmosphere, not just compose an arrangement. Their design trademark is a natural, vertical form, with every flower silhouetted against another. Their cozy shop and extensive greenhouses attract design and gardening aficionados from all over the country. Indeed, it's a must see if you are in the area.

Minimum: $35.00 plus delivery
All major credit cards
Also serves: Ligonier and Pittsburgh

LANCASTER

Nancy Gingrich Floral Designer
NANCY GINGRICH

1352 Harrisburg Pike
Lancaster, PA 17601
(717) 392-2841

Nancy Gingrich's talents as a floral designer are well known throughout the industry. She was one of the florists who created arrangements for Reagan's Inaugural Ball and was invited to design arrangements for the rededication ceremony for the Statute of Liberty in 1986.

In Nancy's work, an American version of the European bouquet, the pastoral unfolds with a powerful impact. Nancy has that rare ability to combine two opposing moods in her work. "I am an artist, but I'm also a craftsman." she says. "Each flower has its own personality, and I must respect that while at the same time conducting all those individual energies into one effect." A one-of-a-kind floral maestro.

She uses plenty of branches: dogwood, forsythia and plum, among others. And by adding a generous helping of lichens, mushrooms and mosses, she imbues her work with a strong vegetative quality that's at once sparse and dynamic.

Minimum: $25.00 plus delivery
All major credit cards
Also serves: Harrisburg, Reading and York

NEW HOPE

The Pod Shop
JOIE STONER

Logan Square Center
New Hope, PA 18938
(215) 862-2037

Mrs. Stoner has been doing lovely natural arrangements for years. "People say my arrangements look like Renaissance bouquets," she told me. "I think that's because there is such a wide variety of material in each piece we do." And similarly, there is always a sumptuous selection of cut flowers in the shop.

At Christmas you might ask about her Williamsburg wreaths. They're frothy, full and romantic.

Minimum: $25.00 plus delivery
All major credit cards
Also serves: Washington Crossing and Yardley

PHILADELPHIA

Includes: Ardmore, Bala-Cynwyd, Bryn Mawr, Gladwyne, Haverford, Merion, Northberth, Penn Valley, Radnor, Rosemont, St. Davids, Villanova and Wynnewood

Robert Mitchell
ROBERT MITCHELL

2006 Hamilton Street
Philadelphia, PA 19130
(215) 557-7565

To state it simply, Robert specializes in good design. He says, "Either you've got it, or you don't, regardless of the period." And clearly other people agree. He's been chosen the Best in Philadelphia by *Philadelphia Magazine* for every year a florist has been cited.

He carries the entire range of flowers, from Southern Hemisphere exotics to Dutch imports, from Hawaiian tropicals to locally grown herbs, wildflowers, garden perennials and annuals. Arrangements are done in baskets, terra-cotta pots or glass vases or on an organic base, such as foam, covered in galax leaves.

If there is one feature characteristic of all Robert's work, it is his elegant, clean design. "I never use Spanish moss—I can't stand dusty or dirty things," he says.

Minimum: $50.00 plus delivery
All major credit cards

Robertson of Chestnut Hill
GEORGE ROBERTSON AND SONS, INC.

8501 Germantown Avenue
Philadelphia, PA 19118
(215) 242-6000

A characteristic of any great organization is its ability to consistently attract talent. Four generations ago Robertson's achieved this goal, and the story continues today. Not only are they able to employ extraordinary talent but many talented men and women, who pursue flowers as a serious hobby, depend upon Robertson's for the perfect flowers that enable them to win the blue ribbon at design contests, such as the Philadelphia Flower Show. The staff here understands the subtle effects made possible by the colors and textures of flowers and foliages, and a startling number of species—at every stage of development from bud to full flower—is always available for them to work with. "We often have seven varieties of rubrum lilies, twenty species of protea, and more orchid varieties than that," Bruce Robertson explains enthusiastically. The combination of thoughtfully applied knowledge and aggressive buying means hardly anything is beyond their scope. *Your* floral imagination is the limit at Robertson's.

The staff's creative abilities are as extensive as their horticultural knowledge. Months before each holiday, the designers submit up to sixty gift ideas, from which ten or so, at various prices, are selected and perfected. One Father's Day they designed a handsome wire topiary mimicking a miniature hot-air balloon. In the "basket," which could be anything from Italian terra-cotta to English ironstone, they planted a selection of green and gray herbs that would, over the summer, grow over the wire frame to resemble the colored stripes of the balloon. So send a gift of one of their holiday creations or a bouquet made of your own choice of flowers.

Minimum: $45.00 plus delivery
All major credit cards
Also serves: The Main Line

Katie Swope & Audrey Nichols
KATIE SWOPE AND AUDREY NICHOLS

730 Andorra Road
Lafayette Hill, PA 19444
(215) 233-1877

These two free-lancers have made a distinct reputation for themselves doing weddings and parties around town, but they are respected for other floral-related projects as well. Katie is designing a line of Christmas plates for Lenox China, while Audrey is known for her selection of antique containers in materials from porcelain to silver.

Their inventive work displays imported and seasonally available garden flowers and foliages in combinations that range from the simple and natural to the spectacular and grand. A simple basket brimming with black-eyed Susans has blackberry vines weaving through the flowers and around the outside of the basket. Blooming clematis curls around the handle of a basket filled with a romantic spring bouquet of fresh tulips, lilac, roses and freesia, heightened with blooming branches. Rose hips tower over and nestle around rubrum lilies set between swaths of native grasses. Katie and Audrey's avid personal attention, combined with their tasteful creativity, results in a sensitive response to any occasion.

Minimum: $50.00 plus delivery
24-hour notice required
Credit to be arranged
Also serves: The Main Line

Trillium
WALLY AND BOOKER HEPPENSTALL

951 Youngsford Road
Gladwyne, PA 19035
(215) 642-8140

The Heppenstalls' shop, located in a town the size of a postage stamp, operates out of the town's former post office. Wally and Booker transformed this large, innocuous space into a dramatic stage for their floral talents, with dark-gray slate, lighted glass cubes, a towering painted black ceiling and black track lights. This postmodern, loftlike interior sets off their very handsome English bouquets. It's a contrast that surprises, and works, which is what Trillium likes to do—delight its customers in a surprising way.

Holiday ideas include fluted champagne glasses overflowing with micro-mini-roses for Valentine's Day. Most everything is done only once, however, Booker says, "Everybody knows each other around here, so I have to be original with each customer." Vases of champagne roses that are supplied by a local grower and known to "hold" for two weeks are very popular. Trillium is especially concerned with the quality of its flowers and knowing how they will do in various circumstances so that they can be appropriately recommended.

Minimum: $35.00 plus delivery
All major credit cards

PITTSBURGH

Alphabetical Order, Ltd.
FRED RUDDOCK

246 South Highland Avenue
Pittsburgh, PA 15206
(412) 661-3413

Fred Ruddock's approach is to emulate the way flowers grow in the garden. His arrangements reflect the influence of English and French country designs, often set in heavy-textured baskets made from root, jute or hemp. Many flowers, such as garden roses, peonies, daffodils and English lavender, are grown specially for the shop and mixed with imported ones. Mosses, lichens and branches are often incorporated into the baskets.

Good ideas here are plentiful, and given a few parameters, such as color and occasion, Alphabetical Order's talented design team can take it from there. "After all," Mr. Ruddock says, "If you can't trust us, then why are you here? You'll get the best deal if I can be flexible. And our work can retain its energy with the freedom of controlled spontaneity."

They enjoy doing seasonal landscapes—terra-cotta trays or low baskets of daffodils, iris, hyacinths and crocuses, with an accent of pussy willow. "But," says Mr. Ruddock, "I love doing all-white arrangements when I can; the dynamics of shading, shadows and texture can be subtle, but powerful."

Alphabetical Order is also known for its selection of concrete garden ornaments, in particular, those in the shape of various animals.

Minimum: $35.00 plus delivery
Credit cards: MasterCard and VISA

Hepatica
RACHEL CHECK

1119 South Braddock Avenue
Pittsburgh, PA 15218
(412) 241-3900

The hepatica is one of the first flowers to bloom in spring, often pushing its lavender petals up through the snow. As a little girl, Rachel would go with her family "hepatica picking" every year. Flowers have always been part of her life.

When just out of college, Rachel traveled to England to work in florists' shops, most notably Constance Spry's. "It's as if that experience brought everything to life that I felt about flowers. It seemed nobody in America was approaching flowers naturally. My experiences in England were the most influential on my work."

This Victorian-style shop is devoted to flowers and has the largest variety of imported and locally grown ones in the Pittsburgh area. Natural, wild and seasonal flora, such as horse chestnut, clematis, peonies and flowering branches are examples of treats to be found at Hepatica whenever local gardeners bring them around.

Arrangements go out in baskets, glass cylinders and bowls or terra-cotta containers.

Minimum: $25.00 plus delivery
All major credit cards

Toadflax
THOMAS BEDGER

5443 Walnut Street
Pittsburgh, PA 15232
(412) 621-2500

Toadflax is more like a home than a store; skirted tables and bookshelves are heaped with

211

Agraria potpourri and candles, antique porcelains, iron urns, terracotta containers and "just a whole lot of oddball things," as Thomas Bedger describes them. It's all elegant, and so are the robust and romantic presentations that are arranged in baskets or glass containers. The work here is straightforward and clean, not trendy. Potted plants or orchids are wrapped in moss.

Toadflax carries delicious gourmet food items as well, and beautiful French ribbons. There's an abundance of good ideas here. Take advantage of the enthusiastic creativity!

Minimum: $35.00 plus delivery
All major credit cards

SCRANTON

➜➤➤✕◀◀

McCarthy Flowers of Scranton
ERIN AND BRIAN MCCARTHY

1225 Pittston Avenue
Scranton, PA 18505
(717) 347-4747

The McCarthys are young, ambitious and efficient. They keep their shop open seven days a week until seven every night, and measure their success by the volume they do: up to two hundred weddings a year. Their arrangements range in style from high-tech contemporary to country bouquets made with flowers that come primarily from South America and Holland. They carry tropicals, but not all varieties.

To enter the shop you walk through the greenhouse, chockfull of foliage and blooming plants. Up to ten designers work right there, so if you visit in person you can watch while you wait. There's a big walk-in cooler from which your choice of cuts is gathered: It could be a dozen rubrum lilies or masses of greenhouse-grown roses. Or how about a hundred white carnations?

Minimum: $15.00 plus delivery
Credit cards: MasterCard and VISA
Also serves: Dunmore, Old Forge and Throop

RHODE ISLAND

NEWPORT

Broadway Florist
PAUL ECKHART

324 Broadway
Newport, RI 02840
(401) 849-4000

An understanding of Newport in general best gives you an idea of the demands and scope of Paul's work. In Newport architectural styles range from the wonderful clapboard colonial houses to the majestic oceanfront mansions to a port full of the world's finest yachts. If you're going to be a successful florist in this town, you have to respect each enclave's taste. And that's just what Paul does.

Colonial houses call for country arrangements in copper kettles or blue and white Spatterware; the mansions need eight-foot grand arrangements "in the 'Dynasty' style"; and the yachts—"well, it depends on who owns them," says Paul. "We usually know what they like, but if not, I'll do a lovely loose arrangement in a seashell."

Last fall he did "Health Baskets": picnic baskets with San Pelligrino water instead of wine, herbal teas, water biscuits and more, with another basket tucked inside filled with fresh autumn flowers. There is a wealth of good and appropriate ideas here, so be sure to ask, and be specific.

213

Minimum: $25.00 plus delivery, which varies according to whether it's by boat or land
All major credit cards

PROVIDENCE

Mount Fuji
RON AND JOANN VESCERA

182 Academy Avenue
Providence, RI 02908
(401) 421-7065

The Vesceras specialize in exotics and tropicals. Their designs are high style with a strong line composition, ranging from Oriental to contemporary. Heliconias, torch ginger, anthuriums and birds-of-paradise are just a few of the flowers they like to use. Their talents extend to European-style designs if a customer specifically requests one.

It's not unusual to see the Vesceras' floral work combined with high-tech metals and plastics, copper tubing or Lucite rods.

Minimum: $25.00 plus delivery
Credit cards: MasterCard and VISA

The Potted Palm
FRANK ROGERS

339 Ives Street
Providence, RI 02906
(401) 421-8530

In this tiny jewel of a shop you won't find a single potted palm—or any potted plants, for that matter. You *will* find exquisite topiaries of herbs, myrtle or boxwood, orchids scattered around and on top of antiques and a profusion of fresh, important flowers that are imported or grown in Mr. Rogers's Connecticut garden.

"Our work is pretty and romantic. I am always inspired by great big heart-wrenching themes, like Camelot, to create moods that are both bigger than life and reminiscent of the small things that make our own lives special," explains Mr. Rogers. Fully blown champagne roses explode out of silver or gilt containers for table arrangements. Nosegays of lily of the valley sparkle in crystal bud vases for the bathroom. Holly, berries and fruits cascade down candelabras for Christmas. It's no wonder Mr. Rogers is in big demand in Newport. Any occasion influenced by his talents will be beautiful and memorable.

Minimum: $25.00 plus delivery
All major credit cards
Also serves: Newport

SOUTH CAROLINA

CHARLESTON

Blumengarten
WERNER GROSS

62 Queen Street
Charleston, SC 29401
(803) 722-4266

Traditional arrangements, in the Constance Spry–style, will always be a must in Charleston, and Werner loves doing them. But with courage and daring he will add a dash of the Far East and, he says, "This is what prompts a second look—even a stare! It's such a joy working with the rare and imported 'blumen' and the natural flora of the Low Country for a most appreciative clientele." He's clearly a pacesetter in Charleston.

European bouquets, whether purchased in this tiny shop or delivered, are always wrapped in transparent cellophane and tied with a deep purple ribbon, which is Mr. Gross's trademark.

Minimum: $25.00 plus delivery
All major credit cards
Also serves: Kiawah Island, Seabrook and Summerville

HILTON HEAD ISLAND

Wildflowers
ROBIN CAVELLA

841 South Island Square
Highway 278
Hilton Head Island, SC 29928
(803) 785-5551

Robin and her associates have a natural ability to design country-style arrangements with a European flair. And they are as adept with tropicals as they are with garden flowers.

Their specialties include cozy arrangements in birds' nests or flowers exploding out of conch shells. They also do wonderful hand-tied bouquets wrapped in multicolored tissue.

Minimum: $25.00 plus delivery
All major credit cards

TENNESSEE

JACKSON

The Flower Patch
CAROL JONES

134 Carriage House Drive
Jackson, TN 38305
(901) 668-1401

W hen Carol opened her shop six years ago, she didn't expect to be as busy as she is today. There is a special flair that goes into every Flower Patch creation. Carol's very pretty, natural bouquets of alstroemeria and Queen Anne's lace appeal to just about everyone. Her goal is to create bouquets that communicate her love for beautiful flowers.

Peach potpourri is popular here, as well as Carol's unusual birch wreaths.

Minimum: $20.00 plus delivery
All major credit cards

KNOXVILLE

By Design
KAE LAKENAN

7003 Sherwood Drive
Knoxville, TN 37919
(615) 588-5065

M s. Lakenan is a free-lancer with a lot of restrictions on single orders; but if you wish to send something really special, her arrangements are spectacular. She has several dedicated growers, people who let her cut whatever and whenever she wants from their gardens. She combines these with wildflowers and Holland imports in asymmetrical, naturally elegant, full arrangements.

A special, though expensive, idea for Christmas are her "Shotgun Wreaths." They are made with red shotgun shells, all of which have been shot, so they have the "hammer" marks on them. The shells are artfully arranged on a wreath frame, glazed with shellac, and accompanied by a card that reads, "365 shots and I didn't get my Christmas goose!"

Minimum: $100.00
One week's notice required
Closed January and February
Credit to be arranged

The Flower Market
CARROL SCHMID AND MARY SPENGLER

4520 Old Kingston Pike
Knoxville, TN 37919
(615) 584-1679

Although The Flower Market began as a cash-and-carry shop for cut flowers, repeated requests from friends for special favors led to its becoming a full-service business. Within five years Carrol and Mary have spanned the width of the floral spectrum, from planning perennial borders to designing one-of-a-kind arrangements.

Unusual though natural arrangements are created in a variety of containers—from rustic baskets to elegant glass cylinders. These combine imported flowers with local ones grown exclusively for The Flower Market. The shop's side patio contains a variety of annual and perennial potted plants, including foxglove, cornflowers and astilbe.

Carrol and Mary are always developing interesting ways to

present flowers and plants. Last fall a popular item was the "Cradle Wreath," a grapevine wreath with a built-in basket in which anything from potted plants to fresh or dried flowers could be placed. Another alternative to cut flowers is the "Market Basket," a natural basket filled with blooming and green plants, creating a garden effect.

Because space is limited, the inventory of gift items is small—but select. They special-order their cachepots from companies like Mottahedeh and their garden statuaries from Robinson Iron, Southern Stone and Hen-Feathers. As you can see, The Flower Market is more than a place to buy cut flowers.

Minimum: $25.00 plus delivery
Credit cards: MasterCard and VISA

MEMPHIS

John Hoover
JOHN HOOVER

2206 Union Avenue
Memphis, TN 38104
(901) 274-1851

J ohn Hoover, a third-generation florist from Dyersburg, Tennessee, revolutionized the Memphis market when he opened a shop there six years ago. He was the first and, until the wholesalers caught up with the trend, the only florist to import Holland flowers. He still imports directly, using no middleman, assuring both quality and a good price. Now he's setting another new trend by suggesting that the farmers in the Memphis area expand their traditional plantings to include the unusual. He explains, "There's so much we could grow right here, especially things you can't get from Holland."

His shop is an old, renovated clapboard house filled with a wealth of terra-cotta, porcelain and iron containers and woven baskets. What struck my eye is the way he decorates his baskets with dried and silk flowers, making them great containers for flowers as well as potpourri. There's a lot of talent and taste here.

Minimum: $25.00 plus delivery
All major credit cards
Also serves: Bartlett, Collierville, Cordova, Germantown and Raleigh

NASHVILLE

The Tulip Tree
JULIA DAVIDSON AND JOE SMITH

6025 Highway 100
Nashville, TN 37205
(615) 352-1466

In Nashville The Tulip Tree has been the chosen florist for some time. Julia and Joe's flowers are romantically arranged and always beautiful. They have the depth of design skills to accommodate their customers' specific desires tastefully and artfully.

The shop is more like a home than a place of business. Fireplaces, chandeliers, marble floors and skirted tables provide a warm backdrop for cachepots filled with seasonally blooming plants, potpourri and a wide range of flowers kept daily, from field flowers to garden roses, perennials and Dutch imports.

Holidays provide an opportunity to develop great gift ideas. For last Valentine's Day a square, French terra-cotta pot with a tiny cherub sitting on the edge held a lovely topiary of minicarnations. The carnations were artfully tied at the top, the mass of stems becoming the perfectly proportioned trunk. I'm always impressed when a florist has the eye, not to mention the courage, to use the carnation, a flower that's gotten such a bad reputation from so much misuse. Hooray, and cheers!

You'll never go wrong at the Tulip Tree, with its profusion of lovely mixed flowers.

Minimum: $35.00 plus delivery
All major credit cards

TEXAS

AMARILLO

H.R.'s Flowers & Gifts
H.R. FULTON

2010 Fourth Avenue
Canyon, TX 79015
(806) 655-2587

A florist in a small town needs not only talent but a warm humility—and not a trace of artistic snobbery. H.R. fits this bill precisely, and for forty years he has been a major force in the floral world in the Panhandle. The demands of his diverse clientele call for his talents to swing from the "round mound" look to massed English-style arrangements. He makes great use of indigenous materials and their decorative potential, but he's sensitive to the potential effect on the recipient. For example, Johnsongrass in a vase is very dramatic, but in the eyes of a local rancher it's a virulent vegetative pest that's almost impossible to get rid of.

Flowers are shipped directly to the shop from California and Hawaii. A local, but very famous, hybridizer of kalanchoe provides H.R.'s shop with wonderful blooming plants. Orchid plants can be ordered with a day's notice. Daily arrangements go out in glass, baskets or terra-cotta. Be specific about what you want, but rest assured your gift is in good hands.

Minimum: $20.00 plus delivery
All major credit cards

AUSTIN

David Kurio Floral Designs
DAVID KURIO

1201-B West Sixth Street
Austin, TX 78703
(512) 480-9426

David Kurio creates lovely, loose Old English bouquets using full-blown roses, gerbera daisies and Queen Anne's lace to dramatic effect. David explains, "We'll find a tree branch covered with lichen and pods and combine that with a cluster of rubrum lilies at the mouth of a vase, with an empty wasps' nest shooting out one side." The effects are exotic and wild. Daily arrangements go out in baskets or glass. "We don't carry a large inventory of vases, because most of our clients bring in their old silver and export ware."

For Christmas last year David dipped baskets in a paraffin chocolate glaze. "You get the luster and feel of chocolate," he says. "Although it's not edible, it's durable." The baskets were filled with masses of flowers, pine cones or nuts.

If you send a plant as a gift, the basket is tied with raffia combined with a smashing cluster of dried flowers in the center of the bow. Everything in this shop is well thought out and artfully finished.

Minimum: $35.00 plus delivery
Credit cards: MasterCard and VISA

CORPUS CHRISTI

Bill Gardner Ltd.
BILL GARDNER

17 Lamar Park Center
Corpus Christi, TX 78411
(512) 857-2598

"We use flowers to indulge people's fantasies," claims Bill Gardner. He combines a bountiful helping of tropicals and Holland imports, usually in baskets, sometimes in glass containers, to create everything from a contemporary look to the more traditional. Often Bill and his associates use containers that disappear into the arrangement, whether it's a vessel covered in galax leaves or fruits and vegetables that have been hollowed out. "I love bromeliads and use them in an arrangement whenever I can," says Bill. "And of course, chili peppers are popular, especially red ones for Christmas and Valentine's Day."

A feeling of restrained grandeur is reflected in his selection of antiques, as well as in his floral sensibility. Neoclassic is Bill's first choice; country French runs a close second, however. "I like anything that's got some fuss to it without a lot of bother," quips Mr. Gardner.

Minimum: $30.00 plus delivery
Credit cards: MasterCard and VISA

DALLAS

Current Flowers
RICHARD HARRINGTON AND STEVEN FOSTER

The Quadrangle
2800 Routh Street, Suite 142
Dallas, TX 75205
(214) 871-1644

Although Richard and Steven have worked together for several years, their store is new. I am not exaggerating when I say they go through a bottle of Windex every week, cleaning the nose prints off the windows. What you see is breathtaking. A strongly architectural environment is the background for an individualistic style, with the flowers taking center stage, whether it's one giant heliconia meticulously placed or a lavish Baroque European bouquet or a wild mix of native grasses and sunflowers. "We see our flowers as what *contemporary* really is—current," says Richard.

They were selected Best Flower Shop in *D Magazine*'s "Best & Worst" issue last January.

Minimum: $25.00 plus delivery
Credit cards: MasterCard and VISA

Preston Flower Market
ALEXIS F. NACCARATO

14902 Preston Road, Suite 1008
Dallas, TX 75240
(214) 386-2988

The Preston Flower Market is a tropical paradise where new ideas and fresh ways of looking at and using flowers and plants abound. The designers here delight in surprise. Unexpected combinations, eccentric presentations and daring visions are the studio's stock-in-trade. Mossed branches are artfully woven into the trunk of azalea topiary trees, or glass cylinders are wrapped in reeds and exotic leaves and then tied with bear grass. Unusual combinations of flowers include miniature pastel calla lilies with anemones, proteas, blooming branches and garden roses.

All of this is done with the purpose of renewing our appreciation of the glorious gift of flowers. The talents at Preston Flower Market can be depended on to achieve this goal tastefully.

Minimum: $30.00 plus delivery
All major credit cards

Zen, A Floral Design Studio
ROSEWOOD HOTELS, INC.

3526 Cedar Springs
Dallas, TX 75219
(214) 526-9736

The talent and dedication in this studio are evident in the dazzling energy the arrangements display. Unique creations range in style from very pretty, romantic bouquets to wild, windswept ones that evoke nature at its purest. Whatever the emotion being expressed, every arrangement is honest, from the heart and not weighed down by the dictates of what is institutionally "correct." Instead, natural instinct is allowed to guide each designer through the choice and breathtaking assembly of flowers.

Flowers are purchased directly from growers all over the world, bypassing all middlemen and wholesalers, thereby ensuring quality, variety and specificity. Local growers keep the studio supplied with sunflowers, zinnias, dahlias and other annuals as well as native grasses and lots of perennials and herbs. The studio is filled with blooming plants, potted perennials, orchids and interesting succulents. Daily arrangements go out in a glass container unless you request one of their wonderful baskets, Pompeiian glass vases or terra-cotta pots. For summer, they've had wooden slat baskets that were rubbed with paints to create an effect like verdigris—the patina that copper and brass achieve.

For holidays, very creative gifts are developed. One Christmas, corporate gift-givers could choose between a della Robbia wreath and one of fresh greens, either one decorated with large Venus flytraps and colorful sedums, weaved through with swaths of raffia and punctuated by a substantial raffia bow. For Mother's Day, a fruit-and-flower topiary artfully combined peaches, blackberry vines and open cranberry-colored roses. The depth and enthusiasm of the talent at Zen is unquestionable.

Minimum: $35.00 plus delivery
All major credit cards

FORT WORTH

Flowers on the Square
BILL BOSTELMANN AND RIC MULLER

311 Main Street
Fort Worth, TX 76102
(817) 870-2888/metro number to Dallas: 429-2888

This is a slick-looking shop where high-tech impressions are perfectly softened by old, brick walls, creating a cool oasis in the Texas heat. Bill makes wonderful European bouquets or, breaking all the rules, will plant a forest of pink cut amaryllis in rock candy.

Bill and Ric carry all the right names in Chardonnay and champagne to send along as gifts with flower arrangements. Wonderful glass containers, terra-cotta pots and baskets fill the shop. They also carry one of the best-looking proprietary potpourris I have ever seen, incorporating entire dried half-slices of baby limes. It has a handsome citrus smell.

Minimum: $30.00 plus delivery
All major credit cards

Petals, Inc.
PAUL TRIPPLEHORN

5001 El Campo
Fort Worth, TX 76107
(817) 738-0934

In this lovely shop, set in an old church of Mediterranean-style pink stucco complete with balustrades and awnings, Paul and his associates create voluptuously European bouquets, Victorian yet sophisticated. Arrangements of imported flowers such as liatris, garden roses, freesia, delphinium and Queen Anne's lace go out in clear glass vases, baskets or terra-cotta containers.

Orchid plants, always a shop staple, are set in moss, with the flower stems supported by curly willow attached with tiny raffia knots. There's a good selection of blooming plants as well. Interesting topiaries, both live and dried, are almost always available.

A well-chosen selection of gifts for the table include oversized Italian fruits and candlesticks, and there are more personal items like Rigaud candles and beautifully wrapped soaps. Petals gets very creative for holiday seasons, so be sure to ask.

Minimum: $30.00 plus delivery
All major credit cards

HOUSTON

David Brown Floral Designs
DAVID BROWN

2625 Colquitt
Houston, TX 77098
(713) 521-1191

One is immediately impressed by the strong architectural style of David's shop. It is bold and handsome, and it comes as no surprise to learn that David's background is in architecture. "I am an architect, and my medium is flowers," he says.

There's nothing precious about his work. Whether he's using tropicals or Holland flowers, it's very stylish. There is a host of tasteful surprises, like the display of "flaming sword" bromeliads in an Old English rustic oak bread basket that you would otherwise expect to see filled with English-garden flowers.

Minimum: $35.00 plus delivery
All major credit cards

Lyman Ratcliff Associates Custom Florist
LYMAN RATCLIFF

91 Dennis Street
Houston, TX 77006
(713) 529-9006

Lots of the floral work here is done with Plexiglas and copper tubing, resulting in a contemporary look. Exotic tropicals are combined with interesting natives. The loyalty of Lyman's following is heartwarming. Everybody I've met in Houston has had nice things to say about him, which is unusual in this competitive business.

Be specific about what you do want and don't want.

Minimum: $25.00 plus delivery
All major credit cards

LUBBOCK

College Flowers
KELLY MARBLE AND RUSSELL PLOWMAN

2213 University Avenue
Lubbock, TX 79410
(806) 765-9329

This shop achieved fame when it was owned by flower maestro Lewis Patillo. When he retired, Kelly and Russell, both working for Mr. Patillo at the time, took the natural course of buying the shop from him.

Kelly and Russell create natural bouquets with a straight-from-the-garden look by combining wildflowers with perennials imported from Holland or bought from suppliers in San Francisco. They do beautiful high-tech designs incorporating tropicals from Hawaii and New Zealand as well. Orchids and a wide selection of blooming plants are kept on hand. Daily arrangements are created in glass cylinders or baskets, and potted plants are set in terra-cotta pots or log baskets dressed with fresh moss and birch twigs. Due to the climate very little is grown locally, but Russell and Kelly take advantage of as much native material as possible, such as honeysuckle and Johnsongrass or grapevines from local vineyards.

A good gift selection of European garden pots, Oriental containers in bronze or porcelain and Italian terra-cotta enhance their floral work.

Minimum: $35.00 plus delivery
All major credit cards

MIDLAND

Ron's Floral Design
DONNA N. SMITH AND RON HUSE

3303 North Midkiff, Suite 115
Midland, TX 79705
(915) 694-7667

For six years Ron and Donna have striven to give Midlanders what they want—within the realm of their integrity. "We're contemporary with a traditional flair," says Ron. They don't carry locally grown flowers, but ship them in from all over the world: orchids from Thailand, tropicals from Hawaii and garden flowers from Holland. They also carry an assortment of foliage and blooming plants and bromeliads.

Daily arrangements go out in glass cylinders or wicker baskets, unless you choose from their selection of Oriental porcelains and Italian terra-cotta or from their line of contemporary containers.

Minimum: $25.00 plus delivery
All major credit cards

Flowers of Distinction
JIMMY HERNANDEZ

1552 West Huisache Street
San Antonio, TX 78201
(512) 733-1392

After years of working in shops, Mr. Hernandez developed such a devoted clientele that he decided free-lancing was the best route to satisfy his personal standards as well as his clients' expectations.

Blends of cultivated wildflowers and indigenous cactus are the hallmark of his breathtaking repertoire. He became famous when he designed a Christmas wreath of these materials for the

230

gates of the LBJ Ranch. Throughout the year, Mr. Hernandez takes advantage of anything local that's in season: magnolias, pink and purple crape myrtles, the purple-hued blooms of the cenizo bush, azaleas and blooming cactus. Of course he supplements his local finds with imported flowers and foliages hand-picked at market.

Mr. Hernandez is intent upon creating arrangements that express his customers' feelings. Give him the minimal guidelines such as color preference, the occasion and the type of container you like, and leave the rest to him.

Minimum: $50.00 plus delivery
Credit to be arranged

The Rose Shop, Inc.
E.B. Castro, Jr., and Manny Luna

1903 San Pedro Avenue
San Antonio, TX 78212
(512) 732-1161

The Rose Shop has a fifty-year tradition of artistry with fresh flowers and of personalized service. The style here is best described as casual elegance in the European manner: light, airy combinations of garden flowers in harmonious colors. Many daily arrangements go out in clear glass. "Not everything has to be arranged," says Manny. "You can hardly beat a glass cylinder filled with simply one kind of flower such as tuberoses or Casablanca lilies." I agree!

Items in their gift selection are purchased with the goal of enhancing the shop's ambience, but you can hardly resist their Italian porcelains or Venetian glass. In-house designs are developed for holidays, so be sure to ask if you're calling around a holiday. Manny and E.B. are refreshingly friendly, making them a delight to do business with.

Minimum: $35.00 plus delivery
All major credit cards

TYLER

Judge, The Florist, Inc.
JAY AND BARBARA WARD

1215 South Broadway
Tyler, TX 75701
(214) 592-6567

This shop runs the gamut from high-style to old-fashioned European-style arrangements. When doing a high-style arrangement, however, the Wards concentrate on the flowers, not on the props. They use everything from tropicals to locally grown wildflowers.

Theirs is a huge operation. On one acre in the middle of town sit several thousand square feet of greenhouse and shop space. In the spring they grow ten thousand tulips. Although the Wards do a generous volume, artistic integrity is as important to them as good value.

For Easter last year they put African violets, freesias and stars-of-Bethlehem in a bird's nest with real quail eggs. Daily gift orders go out in simple glass bowls or cylinders. They are well stocked with Italian terra-cotta and assorted baskets, however, which are also used for charming planted compositions.

Minimum: $35.00 plus delivery
All major credit cards

VICTORIA

Pat Kurtz

P.O. Box 2543
Victoria, TX 77902
(512) 578-6031

I have to admit, I wondered where Pat Kurtz could possibly have acquired the level of skill he exhibits with such tasteful flair. As he explains, "I am a South Texas boy, but I do travel!"

His own huge herb, vegetable and perennial garden yields much of his material, and the rest he culls from the thousands of acres of ranchland he oversees. Natural wreaths of mule deer horns, pepper vines (that can get as large as your forearm), native grasses, tortoise shells, red wasps' nests and flowers make a spectacular display of local materials. Some of the more imaginative of Pat's compositions include old wooden crates filled with shell pink amaryllis, Italian terra-cotta pots brimming over with herbs and perennials, and grapevine baskets overflowing with home-grown vegetables. Clear glass vases are filled with an explosion of wild rose hips, lilies, tulips and grasses, or with romantic hand-tied bouquets of imported European flowers. Everything Pat does is packed with aesthetic surprises.

Bear in mind that Pat, being a free-lancer, does travel quite a bit, but fortunately he works closely with our other entry for Victoria, Le Marche.

Minimum: $50.00 plus delivery
48-hour notice required
Credit to be arranged

Le Marche
PAULA MILLER

1305 East Airline Road
Victoria, TX 77901
(512) 576-4000

Le Marche is a mecca for locals in search of stylish gifts, decorative accessories for home and garden, tableware and gourmet foods and candies. Just a few of the things Paula carries: Paperwhite linens, the entire line of Cherchez aromas from drawer liners to potpourri, wonderful containers for plants and flowers, architectural objects such as terra-cotta busts, and antique furniture including painted pieces. She also carries an extensive collection of china, the most exciting pieces being Bill

Goldsmith's Site Corot botanical china, notably his "Victoria" pattern.

Fortunately for us, Paula's good taste extends to flowers as well. For floral arrangements she works with free-lancer Pat Kurtz, whose work is described separately in the entry preceding this one. Paula's forte is blooming plants. A beautiful gift for any occasion might be some cymbidium orchids and seasonal blooming plants artfully arranged in one of her containers, or a plant sent singly, sensationally dressed with mood moss and your choice of French ribbons or raffia, with a gourmet treat tucked in as an added surprise.

Minimum: $50.00 plus delivery
48-hour notice required
Credit cards: MasterCard and VISA

WICHITA FALLS

Designing Styles
LOLA HAMPTON AND GRADY ROSS

3505 Glenwood
Wichita Falls, TX 76308
Mrs. Hampton: (817) 767-8784
Mrs. Ross: (817) 692-1356

After years of working together on volunteer projects, Grady Ross and Lola Hampton combined their talents in a free-lance floral design business. They do not maintain a shop but specialize in custom floral design, using everything from oncidium orchids to Johnsongrass.

Minimum: $40.00 plus delivery
24-hour notice required
Credit to be arranged

UTAH

SALT LAKE CITY

Bloomingsales
KATY CULP AND SONNIE SWINDLE

Studio: 147 East 800 South
Salt Lake City, UT 84111
(801) 532-5663

Shop: 1358 Foothill Boulevard
Salt Lake City, UT 84108
(801) 532-5663

With a dogged efficiency and a dedication to quality, these women filled a vacuum in fine flowers in Salt Lake City. In their very professional brochure they describe their mission: "To answer your needs with flowers in a variety of types and designs. Orchids. Lilies. Roses. Tulips. Exotic tropicals or simple daisies."

Influenced by English design, the shop carries gardening tools, topiaries, statuary and assorted antique containers, as well as a selection of contemporary vases and loads of handsome baskets. You're free to use your imagination here, but be specific.

Minimum: $25.00 plus delivery
Credit cards: MasterCard and VISA

VERMONT

BURLINGTON

Richard Corbett Flowers
RICHARD CORBETT

100 Shelbourne Street
Burlington, VT 05401
(802) 864-0376

Richard's arrangements are low-key and tasteful. He creates loose bouquets of imported Dutch flowers—stargazer lilies, alstroemeria and freesias—and carefully selected greens, which he wraps in cellophane and ties with gold cording, making the presentation an event in itself. Baskets are chock-full of heather, Swedish ruscus, rubrum lilies, freesias and wax flowers. He keeps a supply of affordable antique containers on hand, too.

Richard finds his only limitation is in using material that people don't find in their own gardens. "Although I love unusual garden and wildflowers, I'm often misinterpreted if I do too much of that," he says. "It's very important to me to know what is appropriate in Burlington." Not only is his perception of local tastes accurate, but his renowned talents take him throughout New England. "I'm like a doctor or a lawyer; when you need me, I'm there!"

Be sure to ask Richard about his charming "make-do" cornucopias, fashioned from antique newspaper and filled with flowers and assorted antique and reproduction toys that he's collected over the years, including alphabet blocks, dolls, wooden trains and gilt nuts. They are whimsical and appropriate not only at Christmas but throughout the year. These go pretty quickly, so get your order in early.

Minimum: $15.00 plus delivery
Credit cards: MasterCard and VISA
Also serves: Charlotte, Colchester and Shelburne

MANCHESTER

The Village Florist
JAY EADE

P.O. Box 785
Manchester Village, VT 05254
(802) 362-4484

Perhaps the spirit of this shop is best captured by the license plate on its delivery van: "VERVE." Lots of "enthusiasm, dash and élan" infuses every exquisite, high-style arrangement. Flowers come directly to the shop from Holland, California and Hawaii. You'll find here a stylized, urban look that often utilizes heliconias, ginger, anthuriums, and other tropicals that best lend themselves to dramatic, flamboyant bouquets. "Our work is not blowsy; instead, perspective converges on a dramatic focal point," explains Ms. Eade.

Special treats are gleaned from local gardeners: clematis, spectacular species of iris, peonies and garden roses. Containers run the gamut from simple glass vases and proprietary ceramics to antique English containers. There are ample creative ideas suitable for every occasion, from serious to fun. "We'll rise to any occasion with papers, ribbons and fanfare! And since we do our own delivery, we can see every order from inception to placement," states Ms. Eade with enthusiastic dedication.

Minimum: $25.00; includes delivery charge for Manchester and Dorset areas
Credit cards: MasterCard and VISA
Also serves: Arlington, Danby, Dorset, Manchester and Stratton

WOODSTOCK

⇶⤫⬿

Woodstock Florists on the Green
PAUL WILDASIN

#1 The Green
Woodstock, VT 05091
(802) 457-4996

Both high-style arrangements of
exotic flowers and sophisticated European garden bouquets flourish
here on The Green. Whichever end of the design spectrum appeals
to your taste, Paul's work is never country or cutsie. He takes
direction from his customers, but says, "I like to have the freedom
to choose specific flowers within the context of the feeling a customer wants to express. It's imperative that I'm allowed to let the
material speak for itself. I don't believe in forcing any flower into
a preconceived design model. That would take the life out of the
arrangement." Clearly, Paul respects the natural beauty of flowers
and feels his responsibility is to enhance that beauty.

Flowers here come from all over the world as well as from
local growers. Paul scans the Vermont woods for lichens, mosses,
tree fungus and other materials appropriate for his designs.

Gift possibilities range from garden furniture to glazed clay
containers and ikebana pots made by local artisans, as well as
unusual baskets. Spectacular dried wreaths are made with unexpected materials such as sea grape leaves, stralitzia, seru and okra
pod.

Minimum: $35.00 plus delivery
Credit cards: MasterCard and VISA
Also serves: Barnard, Bridgewater, Hartland, Plymouth, Pomfret,
Quechee and Reading

VIRGINIA

ALEXANDRIA

The Floral Design Studio
TERRY SMITH

4932A Eisenhower Avenue
Alexandria, VA 22304
(703) 751-0028

With a background in television production, fine arts, and interior design, Terry has the requisite skills that allow his floral talents to rise to any occasion. "I pull all those facets of my past together and focus them on transforming a client's vision into a floral expression," he says.

Terry describes his day-to-day work as European with an Oriental influence, which means his juxtaposition of flowers is unexpected. Balance is achieved in new and surprising ways. An off-center branch of plum blossom is set right by a perfectly positioned red amaryllis.

Terry's range of skills allows him to express a myriad of moods. From his "Zorchie" look, a manipulated, contemporary style using high-tech tropicals, to simple baskets of flowers, Terry can do it all. Be sure to tell him exactly what you want.

Minimum: $30.00 plus delivery
All major credit cards
Also serves: Arlington

CHARLOTTESVILLE

❧❧❧❦❦❦

Elizabeth Booker at Gypsy Springs
ELIZABETH BOOKER

2028 Barracks Road
Charlottesville, VA 22903
(804) 293-3043

Nature is Mrs. Booker's inspiration for flower arranging. Lichens, mosses and woods ferns are often combined with flowers, fruits, plants and bulbs in innovative ways, creating intriguing compositions. Although her arrangements often evoke an English-garden or country house look, a Renaissance touch sometimes sneaks in. Her daily arrangements go out in clever glass containers or baskets or, if you wish, in *your* favorite silver bowl or heirloom crystal epergne.

Mrs. Booker is known throughout this cosmopolitan university community for going beyond the expected. When a little boy who loves flowers was bedridden in the hospital, she created a forest setting that made room for a popular toy car that can travel over obstacles. The medical staff marveled at the fun he had as his car sped through the sylvan setting on his bed covers. Hearing this story and others, I couldn't help wondering why she went to such great lengths, to which she philosophically replied, "Everybody has their own style. I try very hard to personalize every arrangement, to create for the individual."

Although Mrs. Booker is a free-lance artist, she can provide an assortment of foliage and blooming plants, as well as a variety of unusual orchids. When such potted plants are chosen as gifts, the pots are decoratively wrapped in sheet moss caught up with a raffia bow.

Minimum: $50.00 plus delivery
48-hour notice required
Credit to be arranged

The Gilded Lily
JAMES HOLLINGSWORTH

104 12th Street, NW
Charlottesville, VA 22903
(804) 296-2199

In what used to be the red brick kitchen of a large old summer house, Jim creates tasteful fantasies, one after the other. As one of his clients described his talents, "He's the only person I know who can combine roses with rutabagas and make it divine."

Jim's service is personal. Flowers sent to somebody in the horse world are automatically wrapped in cellophane and ribbons that match the recipient's racing colors. Orchids are potted in old hollow stumps with lichens and mushrooms. "I want to keep that woodsy feel. It's so appropriate here," says Jim, who is definitely out to dazzle *and* to please.

Arrangements are natural, taking advantage of everything local and in season.

Minimum: $30.00 plus delivery
All major credit cards
Also serves: Culpeper and Orange

LYNCHBURG

Laughon-Patterson
NANCY PATTERSON AND MEG LAUGHON

1303 Langhorne Road
Lynchburg, VA 24503
(804) 384-8528

Nancy and Meg are free-lancers and consequently do a lot of custom work. They are known for their loose, gardeny arrangements that take great advantage of lots of native material. "I like mixing arbelia, joe-pye weed and zinnias we cut from our garden. Meg and I both have large cutting gardens for our business," Mrs. Patterson says.

They also import a great many flowers, though they try to be seasonal; greens and berries at Christmas and garden-fresh flowers in the summer.

Minimum: $35.00 plus delivery
Credit to be arranged

MIDDLEBURG

The Corner Garden
SALLY BOLTON

P.O. Box 1645
Middleburg, VA 22117
(703) 687-5949

Sally spends a lot of time doing landscape design, so not only does she really know her plants, but she has a terrific supply of garden-fresh perennials and annuals to choose from as well. When you combine a love for growing things with a talent for arranging them, both of which Sally has, the result is exceptionally rewarding for everybody. Her arrangements show more depth than one with just imports. And the look is warmer and friendlier. Be sure to ask about The Corner Garden's wonderful gourmet food baskets. All the food is fresh from the oven, and the wines are from local vineyards.

Minimum: $30.00 plus delivery
Credit to be arranged, with local references
Also serves: Aldie, Delaplane, Marshall, The Plains and Upperville

Devonshire
NELSON HAMMELL, PETE HAWKINS AND JOANN SHEA

7 South Madison Street
Middleburg, VA 22117
(703) 687-5990

"We travel frequently so we don't get stale," says Mr. Hammell. Their efforts keep their floral talents au courant and their garden and flower accessories replenished. Just some of the things you'll find: books about flowers from all over the world; hand-carved roosters, pigs and rabbits; urns of every imaginable material, both old and new; fabulous birdhouses and cages; lots of fancy finials; terra-cotta pots; and baskets, baskets, baskets! Mr. Hammell told me, "We have the ordinary ivy topiaries, but also two-, three-, and five-tiered myrtle and rosemary topiaries we grow in our greenhouse."

Clearly of neoclassic persuasion, their arrangements are georgeous and diverse. While one arrangement will be one of delicate sensibility, another can be so powerful its beauty will take your breath away.

Minimum: $35.00 plus delivery
Credit cards: MasterCard and VISA
Also serves: Aldie, Delaplane, Leesburg, Marshall, The Plains and Upperville

NORFOLK

Flowers — W. Walsh
MARGO CAGLE, AIFD

1907 Colonial Avenue
Norfolk, VA 23517
(804) 625-6415

Margo bought this established business six years ago and revitalized it. Her advertising jingle says it: "For those who desire a touch of artistic imagination." Her work is style-conscious whether she's doing a traditional soft, airy garden arrangement or a high-tech manipulation incorporating painted materials or a contemporary look combining pods and tropicals.

Daily arrangements go out in baskets or in glass, ceramic or acrylic containers. Be sure to let her know exactly what you want.

Minimum: $30.00 plus delivery
All major credit cards
Also serves: Chesapeake, Portsmouth and Virginia Beach

RICHMOND

Four Seasons
BILL ELLIS

1200 West Main Street
Richmond, VA 23220
(804) 355-4584

Flowers as an exact art form is a subject that's been debated for years. At Four Seasons it is understood that great design is exacting, and the team here works very hard to express the customer's personality as well as to adhere to the shop's own demanding standards.

The designers can work within their customer's preferences, creating, for example, a bouquet of loose, mixed flowers, but their trademark is an arrangement with a sculptured, highly designed look.

Minimum: $20.00 plus delivery
Credit cards: MasterCard and VISA

Vanity Fair Flowers
DENNIS BRUMBACK

320 Libbie Avenue
Richmond, VA 23226
(804) 288-6009

Being as popular as he is, Dennis is so busy that he never seems to have time to get everything done. He says, "If you saw my shop . . . ughhhh! And my windows are always half done, but the customer comes first." Dennis takes the necessary time to attend to every little detail for his clientele. Papier-mâché angels are carefully dressed with his own dried flowers; delicious heart-shaped homemade cherry tarts are combined with a spring bouquet for Valentine's Day. These are just a few examples of the creative gifts that Dennis puts together.

And he always seems to be ten steps ahead of local tastes. "By the time a new idea is big here, I'm already tired of it; but I'm grateful for any aesthetic progress. For example, I'm so tired of the mixed look. Why not huge vases of one flower—gobs and gobs of the same thing, such as a low three-foot rectangular mass of roses for a centerpiece?" Sounds great to me.

Minimum: $25.00 plus delivery
Credit cards: MasterCard and VISA

ROANOKE

Greenway Court Flowers
KERRY McCARTY AND HARRIETTE McDONALD

1201 South Jefferson
Roanoke, VA 24016
(703) 981-1633

Kerry does a Virginia version of the English-garden look. With Holland imports he combines locally grown treats like black-eyed Susans, goldenrod and zinnias provided by a local farmer's market. He says, "By incorporating what grows outside my back door with exotics, I can achieve a great diversity of style without compromising the nature of the flowers."

Minimum: $25.00 plus delivery
Credit cards: MasterCard and VISA
Also serves: Salem and Vinton

VIRGINIA BEACH

Flowers by Sandra
SANDRA BAYLOR

171 Pinewood Road
Virginia Beach, VA 23451
(804) 428-5440

An energetic and enthusiastic florist in this part of the country can add up to something special. The climate here is cold enough for plants that need a hefty frost to set up a bloom, such as peonies, but warm enough for camellias and crape myrtle. And Sandra Baylor is just that sort of rare florist who makes the effort to take advantage of all the aesthetic possibilities of the native foliage and garden flowers growing around her. She doesn't rely just on imported flowers. Consequently, each one of her arrangements takes on a vibrant individuality.

Her talents are expansive, ranging from contemporary to traditional designs. "There isn't anything I won't try," exclaims Ms. Baylor. And her creativity is delightfully surprising. For Thanksgiving she's known for her Arcimboldo-style turkeys— made completely from fruits and vegetables, and perfect on a bed of straw or silver platter. The planted baskets she composes are also great for gifts.

Minimum: $35.00 plus delivery
Credit to be arranged

WILLIAMSBURG

Williamsburg Floral
ELGIN MORRIS

701-K Marrimac Trail
Williamsburg, VA 23185
(804) 229-9844

Elgin has two stores, each of which reflects a specific style. One is devoted to a traditional Williamsburg look and country style, while the other is more contemporary. His designers float from one to the other, and consequently their skills are kept finely tuned.

For both shops many materials are grown locally and combined with imports. Natives include honeysuckle, wisteria, silver maple, boxwood, rose hips, magnolia, holly and cotton and okra pods. This is one of the most horticulturally diverse areas of the country, and Elgin is intelligently enthusiastic about the aesthetic potential in all things growing around him.

Combine this abundant flora with Elgin's creativity, and you've got a very special shop.

Minimum: $25.00 plus delivery
Credit cards: MasterCard and VISA
Also serves: Lightfoot

WASHINGTON

SEATTLE

Elise Cole
Elise Cole

3826 41st Avenue, NE
Seattle, WA 98105
(206) 525-9648

Elise's commitment to creative expression and her dedication to flowers is best communicated by her own description of her business: "I design and arrange everything myself. I am not interested in lots of designers working for me because I want to spend my time arranging the flowers, not managing a crew."

She combines garden-fresh flowers with imports in a natural, loose manner and sets them in either clear glass or baskets. Elise's respect for the natural movement inherent in each flower is obvious from one look at her arrangements. "I start each arrangement differently, carefully listening to what each flower or foliage is saying," says Elise. Unquestionably it's this emotional and spontaneous relationship with her materials that makes all her work so naturally lovely.

Minimum: $75.00 plus delivery
Credit to be arranged
Also serves: Bellevue and Mercer Island

Robert Hutchinson
ROBERT HUTCHINSON

Sheraton Hotel
1400 Sixth Avenue
Seattle, WA 98101
(201) 343-7188

As Robert says, "I like to take license in summing up what a customer wants." He prefers to do stylish bouquets of cottage-garden flowers, incorporating a few tropicals, but he can be dramatically creative if specifically asked.

The shop's handsome and muted taupe and marble interior serves as a stylish backdrop for the flowers. The spotlight is focused on Robert's floral talents. It's a well-deserved spot on center stage, not cluttered with a lot of giftware.

Although he maintains a select inventory of affordable antique containers, daily gift arrangements normally go out in baskets (typically, reproduction Japanese), glass bubbles or cylinders.

Minimum: $20.00 plus delivery
All major credit cards
Also serves: Bellevue, Edmonds, Mercer Island, Redmond and Renton

Master Florist of Seattle
LOIS AND JAMIE SUNDSTROM

2134 Third Avenue
Seattle, WA 98121
(206) 448-7673

Tropicals combined with natural materials such as driftwood, rocks, moss and bark and set in ceramic or glass containers create the strong line in floral sculpture that Master Florist of Seattle is known for. It's a style that finds its roots in ikebana, but with a northwestern twist. Floral techniques, such as tufting, layering and pillowing of materials are often employed to spotlight the focal point of the arrangement, usually at the lip of the container, which may be accentuated by sheets of birch bark or a large tropical blossom. The movement in the design emanates from this central point. The energy of the vertical motion draws the eye up and around the entire piece.

The shop doubles as an art gallery, and the flowers dynamically complement the paintings in each exhibition.

Minimum: $20.00 plus delivery
All major credit cards
Also serves: Bellevue, Mercer Island and Renton

WEST VIRGINIA

CHARLESTON

Walker's Flower Shop
JOE WALKER

1309 East Washington Street
Charleston, WV 25301
(304) 346-7622

In many places it's easy for florists to be overwhelmed and confused by the change in floristry that has been occurring in this country. Often they flounder and wonder why what used to work doesn't suffice anymore. To solve the problem of profitability, many florists expand their business to include other services, a move that usually doesn't improve the quality of their floristry.

But hooray for Joe Walker! Finding himself confronted with a more sophisticated customer, he closed his original store and focused his efforts on the quality of his flowers and the style of his designs. His new shop has come through the transition with its quality intact. His goal is to create lovely, natural, loose and airy English-style bouquets. "Four years ago we took a whole new avenue. We're more quality-oriented than quantity-concerned," he says.

Flowers are imported directly from all over the world and combined with treats from local gardens. "We get dill, cockscomb, marigolds, zinnias and flowering branches from local sources. Unfortunately, we don't have a great supply of local garden roses yet."

Since the shop's main focus is on flowers, very little is done with giftware or foliage plants. A lot of containers are made in house. Disposable containers are covered with mosses and lichens collected from Joe's property. He carries a nice selection of clear-glass containers and baskets as well.

Minimum: $25.00 plus delivery
All major credit cards

WHEELING

John Diekman & Sons

Floral Avenue
Wheeling, WV 26003
(304) 242-6000

This family business, started in 1900 as a wholesale flower distributor, has expanded to include a garden center as well as a retail flower shop. Although the inventory of materials is expansive, there are a few items that just aren't big in Wheeling. "We tried growing planted herbs, but they just didn't sell. And expensive flowers like rubrum lilies or heliconia aren't too popular either," says Rose Potts, the shop manager. "We're introducing gerbera daisies, protea and cut stems of cymbidium orchids; these types of flowers are beginning to be accepted." Hooray for the innovative thinkers at John Diekman & Sons!

Styles range from traditional bouquets of affordable flowers to loose and gardeny arrangements. Work goes out in glass vases, baskets or plastic containers. These people are more than willing to help, so feel free to express your desires.

Minimum: $20.00 plus delivery
Credit cards: MasterCard and VISA

WISCONSIN

MILWAUKEE

The Flower Studio, Ltd.
LARRY A. MASTERS, AIFD AND MICHAEL J. HUEBNER, AIFD

6933 North Port Washington Road
Milwaukee, WI 53217
(414) 228-9200

What a dramatic store! Black and white tiles on the ceiling and black track lights towering above gray carpeting create the exciting feeling you get backstage before the curtain rises. Larry and Michael are adept at setting the stage for any performance. It's not unusual for them to fill four-foot cylinder vases with cranberries. They say, "We love to hit the ceiling, especially on buffet tables or anytime we can."

Otherwise their look is light and loose. A restrained use of flowers accentuates the design aspects. "When we can, we love to go contemporary," Larry explains. Fruits and vegetables, such as sliced pomegranate, artichoke or cranberries, are combined with fresh flowers and curly willow, bittersweet or other branches. Larry and Michael have a wealth of native materials and garden flowers grown locally for the shop and, of course, they import European flowers.

They make animals of preserved Eucalyptus leaves: ring-necked pheasants, teddy bears and frogs, to name a few. The leaves vary in color from rust to brown to maroon; the color gradations are intricate.

For the hunter who's had no luck during the season, they make moose and deer heads out of cardon "puffs"—they have to be seen to be really appreciated. They make for a fashionably amusing above-the-fireplace decoration.

The enthusiasm here is palpable, and a pleasure to get caught up in.

Minimum: $35.00 plus delivery
All major credit cards

SHOREWOOD

The Shorewood Florist
JIM MANDERS

4600 North Wilson Drive
Shorewood, WI 53211
(414) 332-7060

Mr. Manders's basic design premise was best described when he told me, "Every designer has a floral philosophy. Unlike so many florists who strive for an individual style, I have always preferred to present arrangements that correctly reflect the tastes and ideas of my clients. To me, the customer is the best source of ideas—we listen, and interpret what the client wants." When you place an order here, you speak directly with a designer, so be sure to explain what you want.

Although Jim has had extensive training and he's very professional, his work is not contrived or commercial. His arrangements, whatever genre, are drenched with soulful expression, a prerequisite for good floral design.

The shop is filled with gifts and accessories, as well as tasteful, specially made containers. Last Valentine's Day Jim tied a handsome red metal bow to a wicker basket, which he filled with tulips or a grand amaryllis plant.

Minimum: $35.00 plus delivery
All major credit cards

WYOMING

CODY

❧❧❧❧❧

Forget-Me-Not Floral
JOYCE HUDSON

1012 12th Street
Cody, WY 82414
(307) 587-4935

Although traditional flowers such as pixy carnations, baby's breath and fuji mums are used in arrangements here, they are loosely arranged in an attempt to mimic a wildflower look. Flowers must be shipped in, primarily from Denver, taking two days to get to Cody. Such technical restrictions dictate a reliance on long-lasting flowers, hence the lack of delicate perennials that are so readily available elsewhere in the country.

A warm and personalized service makes this shop a pleasure to do business with. They will deliver, for a reasonable charge, to many of the resort ranches up to fifty miles away, and to most of the motels in Yellowstone Park.

Minimum: $20.00 plus delivery
All major credit cards
Also serves: Yellowstone Park hotels

CANADA

BRITISH COLUMBIA

VANCOUVER

The Flower Show
JULIA DODD AND SUSAN DE WOLF WILLIAMS

4430 West 10th Avenue
Vancouver, BC V6R 2H9
(604) 224-3711

The Flower Show began five years ago with a wide range of flowers in a marketlike setting. Now Dodd and Williams's floral talents cover all styles from contemporary to country, although they are best known for their English-style bouquets in baskets and glass containers.

All three of their stores offer a wide selection of flowers, including tropicals, seasonally available garden flowers, French and Dutch imports, blooming and foliage plants and potted perennials and topiaries. Whatever your choice, the flowers are "allowed to speak for themselves," says Julia. You should consider the expansive range of possibilities and be specific in your choice.

Minimum: $30.00 plus delivery
All major credit cards

Thomas Hobbs
TOM HOBBS

2127 West 41st Avenue
Vancouver, BC V6M 1Z6
(604) 263-2601

Tom's aesthetic dazzles with bundles of small terra-cotta pots filled with lilies-of-the-valley; baskets brimming over with poppies, ranunculus, French tulips and full-blown roses; and terra-cotta trays of mixed herbs or blooming perennials. Those are just a few of the highlights that brighten his extensive repertoire, which has given his thirteen-year-old business that most sought-after recognition, selection as one of *W* magazine's suggested Christmas gift sources. The surprising bonus is that everything Tom does is a good value, which is why he sells out of everything quickly—so place your orders early.

His shop, in a restored bank building with towering neoclassical columns, is filled with specimen plants and buckets of garden flowers, as well as orchid plants and bulbs that he grows in his rooftop greenhouse. Daily orders are done in either clear glass, wicker or roughly hewn, handsome baskets, but there is also an extensive choice of Italian terra-cotta. Tom overlooks no detail in expressing his creative respect for the natural world. For example, if you choose a simple terra-cotta pot for a gift of rubrum lilies or an amaryllis, you can be sure the pot has been exposed to the weather long enough to have just the right amount of algae coloration.

Tom's talent extends to his second shop, called the Well-Furnished Garden, which is filled with English garden furniture, statues, pergolas, pots and other such items. As a life-style journalist said, "Tom's international reputation has become a cachet of style that rules people's lives." Give Tom your basic parameters of budget and occasion and leave the rest to him.

Minimum: $35.00 plus delivery
All major credit cards

ONTARIO

TORONTO

Blossoms
DEBORAH REID

1 Rosenwood Avenue
Toronto, ON M4W 1Y5
(416) 960-8603

Blossoms is best known for its loose and natural English-style arrangements that combine seasonally available garden flowers such as roses, hydrangeas, peonies and lavender with Dutch and French imports like tulips, freesia and anemones.

Deborah and her associates are always taking advantage of aesthetic opportunities. Artistic touches of moss enhance the trunks of standard azalea topiaries; duck-shaped topiaries are rolled in scented potpourri; wooden crates painted mallard green with natural rope handles become decorative packaging for dried or live topiary trees; the cracks of roughly hewn baskets are accented with assorted mosses, making a wonderful container for flowers or seasonally available orchids.

Although Blossoms's small size (five hundred square feet) restricts its inventory, the selection of gifts is exciting. Attractive containers from Cindy's Bows in California and Ronaldo Maia's shop in New York, as well as various potpourris and herb wreaths, are also available.

Minimum: $45.00 plus delivery
All major credit cards

Demarco-Perpich Design Inc.
PETER DEMARCO AND GARY PERPICH
1096 Young Street
Toronto, ON M4W 2L6
(416) 967-0893

Opulent bouquets of imported Dutch and French flowers combine ranunculus, lilies-of-the-valley, full-blown roses, delphinium, lupines and lilies with carefully selected unusual foliage, such as wild cucumber or mimosa spilling over the sides of clear glass containers or baskets. "We use fruits on the vine whenever we can. We use grapes, crab apples, blackberries and rose hips," says Peter. Every arrangement nestles one glorious flower next to another in abundant splendor.

There is a wide assortment of potted blooming plants, which go out in terra-cotta unless otherwise specified. Choices include seasonal orchids, freesia, spring bulbs in saucers or crates, amaryllis, lilies and primroses, to name a few.

Topiaries (both dried and live) and special holiday creations are offered. Last Christmas, for example, a gilded square clay pot contained a selection of glistening sugar-coated grapes, sugar plums and nectarines built into the shape of a Christmas tree. In this shop tasteful and traditional ideas are given new life with a controlled dash of modern style.

Minimum: $45.00 plus delivery
All major credit cards

OTTAWA

Scrim's Florist
262 Elgin Street
Ottawa, ON K2P 1L9
(613) 232-2466/-1733

Scrim's has been the traditional favorite in town for more than a century, and while old, it stays up-to-date. Scrim's caters to a quality-conscious clientele concerned with long-lasting flowers of good value. For this reason, paper-white narcissus are sold only as cut flowers and not in bulb form. Terra-cotta pots are available, but plants usually go out in baskets, unless otherwise specified. Blooming plants are of the traditional reliable sort, such as cyclamen, azaleas and chrysanthemums. Bulb plants, such as tulips, hyacinths and daffodils, are offered when in season, usually beginning near the end of January. There is a good selection of foliage plants as well.

Flowers are shipped in from all over the world, both tropicals and garden perennials. There is no local source of garden-grown roses or field flowers, but summer annuals such as zinnias and snapdragons are seasonally available. The gift line extends to affordable crystal, baskets and ceramics. For holidays, Scrim's relies on wire-service creations.

Within this traditional framework, the first priority of Scrim's friendly and obliging staff is to please the customer. Keep your plans straightforward and be specific with your choice of flowers, container and presentation.

Minimum: $35.00 plus delivery
All major credit cards

QUEBEC

MONTREAL

Fleurs Gilbert, Inc.
GILBERT LANOUTTE

4259 St. Catherine's Street
Westmount, PQ H3Z 1P7
(514) 932-5546

Gilbert's arrangements are filled to overflowing with flowers. His disciplined style conveys a sensibility that is opulent and sophisticated, never country or weedy. The integrity of the flowers is displayed; nothing is contrived. Daily arrangements go out in your choice of clear glass or wicker, and a tasteful selection of Oriental porcelains is also available.

Tropicals and garden flowers from all over the world are always available here to meet Gilbert's artistic vision. Blooming plants such as kalanchoe, seasonal orchids and bulbs, topiary azaleas in the standard form and cyclamen are placed in terra-cotta pots unless otherwise specified. An eye for quality and keen sensitivity for the occasion, combined with Gilbert's concern for the customer, result in lovely and appropriate bouquets.

Minimum: $50.00 plus delivery
All major credit cards

Van Horn & Roberge, Inc.
DANIEL ROBERGE

1448A Sherbrooke West
Montreal, PQ 833 1K4
(514) 284-0065

Thirteen years ago Daniel Roberge and the late Eric Van Horn opened their shop. They were the first in this town to display flowers in their natural splendor, and ever since the staff has dazzled Montreal with their creative spirit. Their designs are strongly influenced by the English garden, specifically the perennial border. Although their arrangements are sophisticated, a wild spirit imbues them. Daniel takes advantage of imported flowers as well as locally grown, seasonally available ones such as roses, phlox, delphinium, blooming branches, herbs and annuals. Daily arrangements go out in your choice of clear glass containers or baskets.

A carefully chosen selection of blooming plants is always available. Orchid plants are tastefully presented in terra-cotta. Fresh-flower topiaries are constructed on request, but living topiaries of ivy, boxwood and azalea are a mainstay. Although the staff here is sensitive to holiday themes, no specific gift ideas are developed. Give Van Horn & Roberge the essential parameters of budget and occasion and leave the details to the very talented staff.

Minimum: $35.00 plus delivery
All major credit cards

GLOSSARY

Defining botanical terms, floral styles or perhaps anything to do with plants always invites spirited controversy. As a botanist by training, and having studied under one of our country's great taxonomists, I've witnessed firsthand the endless debates about what family a plant ought to belong to. These arguments center on how to weigh certain criteria in determining a plant's classification. The lily family, for example, is always a topic of debate: Should amaryllis and agave (century plant) be considered part of that family, or should they be split off to form a family of their own? And defining floral styles—such a task conjures up all kinds of fallout as a result of the ambiguity that is inherent in expressing verbally anything visual.

So when my publisher asked me to write a glossary, I shivered inwardly while outwardly exclaiming that surely everybody knows what oasis and lead bows are. A random telephone survey ensued, and I was proved wrong. So here I am sticking my neck out with a glossary. It's not the final word, and shouldn't be. After all, the process of living involves learning, inventing and accumulating new ideas and ways of doing things. Knowledge, like styles, changes, and with these changes evolve new and different ways of talking about things—like flowers.

Thus the intent of this glossary is to provide definitions of terms and descriptions of styles that are commonly used now, as well as brief biographical descriptions of the famous floral designers who are mentioned in this handbook. Undoubtably definitions of things like oasis and raffia will not change with time; nonetheless, all the design styles will most assuredly take on mutations as time passes. At least for now with the help of this glossary we can communicate a little better in the language of *Fine Flowers by Phone.*

Boldfaced terms or names within an entry signify that those terms or names are themselves defined in this glossary.

AIFD. Abbreviation for American Institute of Floral Design. Qualifications for membership are extensive, including rigorous tests and numerous demonstrations. The organization holds the usual conventions and contests. Its meaning and value has been open to debate. Although every member is technically proficient—that is, highly skilled in mechanics and jargon—membership is not a guarantee of artistic ability or taste. Nevertheless, all members should be granted respect for their accomplishment. At the same time, it should be noted that many of the best florists in this country are by choice not members.

ANNUALS. Plants that complete their life cycle in one year or less. They burst from seed, bloom for a season and then are killed by the first hard frost. To achieve their effect the next year, seeds must be restarted. Examples include petunias, zinnias, sunflowers, and cosmos.

ARCIMBOLDESQUE. Either a topiary or animal or human figure constructed out of fruits and vegetables, sometimes incorporating herb plants. Named after a sixteenth-century Italian court painter who developed a portrait invention, the "composite head," in which witty combinations of fruits, vegetables, fish, flowers and other objects were fitted together into head-and-shoulder figures. The flora and fauna were painted with meticulous realism. His best-known series of paintings are the *Four Seasons* and the *Elements*.

BIEDERMEIER. A nineteenth-century style of furniture, interior and floral design that has recently enjoyed a resurgence in this country. The floral arrangements, reflecting the German desire for orderliness, harmony and neatness, are characterized by a semispherical shape and a perfectly smooth surface—that is, with no spaces between the flowers. The dense bouquet may be comprised of concentric rings of similar flowers: a ring of tulips around a ring of alliums around a ring of miniature carnations around a ring of roses, and so on. Or it may simply be of analogous or monochromatic colors. If the flowers are arranged in relatively tight bud the bouquet changes character each day as the blossoms open, but still keeps its smooth, spherical character.

BIENNIALS. Plants that complete their life cycle in two years. From seeds they produce leafy growth the first year, flower in the second year, and die soon after. Examples include Canterbury bells, foxglove, hollyhocks and forget-me-nots.

CLUSTERING. Clumping many specimens of one variety of a flower into an arrangement, at the same or different heights. If you take a handful of tulips and place it into any arrangement, you are clustering tulips.

FLEUR COWLES. American editor, author, painter and diplomat. She created and edited *Flair* magazine; was an associate editor of *Look;* wrote the authorized biographies of Salvador Dali and Evita and Juan Perón; gained international acclaim as a painter, often depicting flowers; and represented the United States at the coronation of Queen Elizabeth II. Cowles's unique style in floral design is beautifully portrayed in her book *Flower Decorations: A New Approach to Flower Arranging* (New York: Villard Books, 1985). She strongly emphasizes experimentation while avoiding eccentricity, and simultaneously disregards professional rules about measured heights and widths. She believes that instinct, when guided by love and humor, inevitably produces lovely arrangements. Finally, she values the effect of massing flowers. She'll create dense mosaics of flowers of all the same genus (for example, different varieties of daffodils) or of flowers of all different kinds. Her look is simple, bold and artfully dramatic, often incorporating a botanical pun.

DELLA ROBBIA. Named after a fifteenth-century Italian family of craftsmen famous for introducing the possibility of painting colors onto pottery, breaking the barriers that had previously separated ceramics from other arts.

In flower arranging, the term implies the decorative use of fruits in garlands, wreaths, swags and other foliage decorations. An example is oranges and lemons artfully interspersed into a garland of bay leaves.

ENGLISH DESIGN. Seemingly uncontrived arrangements composed of a textural kaleidoscope of garden-type flowers and foliages, from monochromatic to multicolored. Design variations, determined by the type of flowers used and the method of arranging them, express a range of moods from formal to casual.

Spontaneous combinations of meadow flowers and wildflowers with herbs and roadside grasses convey a cozy country feeling, hence the term *English country bouquets.* More studied combinations, using much grander and more important flowers such as lilies, tulips, roses and lilac in conjunction with cultivated garden foliages, make for more formal arrangements. While Old World, Renaissance and Edwardian arrangements are variations on the same uncontrived theme, they are not necessarily of British descent. These arrangements use flowers that were both available and popular during their respective historical periods.

Today, Victorian bouquets are more tightly packed and romantic in feeling than the typical English-garden bouquet, making use of opulent flowers such as fully blown garden roses, ranunculuses, tulips, campanulas, lilies and peonies. The historical significance of the Victorian movement in flower arranging involved the passionate imposition of strict rules and regulations, including dictates on the size and shape of vase to be used.

EUROPEAN OR FRENCH STYLE. These terms imply a more cultivated restraint than the "from-the-garden" look of English bouquets. French country bouquets are different from their English counterparts only in their predominant use of flowers more closely associated with the French countryside, such as red poppies or mustard. Although the types of flowers and the emotional expression of each style may overlap, the visual effects can be distinct enough to warrant different terms. With the internationalization of available flowers today, these terms are becoming somewhat academic.

EUROPEAN TIED BOUQUETS. Like **wrap bouquets** in that they come without a container. In addition, however, all the stems are placed together, tied at their narrowest point and then cut to the same length. Thus the weight is perfectly distributed, so the bouquet can stand up on its own, like a many-legged tripod. A major benefit of this technique is that a huge massed bouquet of flowers so tied can be gripped in one hand. And the stems look very pretty when placed in a clear glass vase.

Like wrap bouquets, the stems should be carefully recut and placed immediately in water.

FLEMISH STYLE. Inspired by the paintings of seventeenth-century Dutch and Flemish artists such as Brueghel, Van Huysman, Verendael and Steen, in which all the elements of the floral still life were painted in painstaking detail. A perfect example is the painting on the cover of this book.

Sumptuous combinations of all sorts of flowers and foliages, and sometimes fruits, birds, butterflies and bugs, are juxtaposed to strike a tenuous balance between opposing moods—formal and whimsical, romantic and restrained, contrived and spontaneous—creating an almost spiritual effect.

FLOWERING BRANCHES. Branches of trees or bushes cut in spring, while they are in flower, to be used in arrangements. Examples include dogwood, apple, quince, forsythia and pear. At other times of the year, particularly in the fall, when dogwood, maple and beech turn bright red and gingko turns a luminous yellow, branches may also be used decoratively.

HERBS. Plants best known for their culinary or medicinal uses or for their aromatic qualities. Some (rosemary, thyme lavender, scented geranium) are perennials; others (dill, basil) are annuals. For years herbs have also been used for decoration, as in wreaths, topiaries and potpourri. Today their flowers and foliage are becoming increasingly popular in flower arrangements and bouquets.

HIGH-STYLE ARRANGEMENTS. Strong line compositions with an accentuated focal point. It can be argued that the sources of this style are **ikebana** (for the strong line effect) and fifteenth- and sixteenth-century Dutch and Flemish paintings, particularly those of Huysum (for the strong focal point). Arrangements are often bold, and never soft. Flowers are sometimes combined with props, such as metal or Plexiglass rods. Sometimes leaves, and even the flowers themselves, are twisted, wrapped or bent around one another. This is probably the closest flower arranging comes to sculpture and is the antithesis of the natural garden style and the casual bouquets reminiscent of the uncontrived Renaissance styles. See also **ikebana, minimalist arrangements.**

IKEBANA. The disciplined art of Japanese flower arranging, characterized by a linear, sparse design and steeped in symbolism. Ikebana became popular during the 1910 fad for all things Japanese. Its form has recently had dramatic influence on **high-style arrangements** in this country.

IMPORTS. Flowers and plants brought into this country from Mexico and overseas. Major sources of imported flowers include Holland, France, Israel and South and Central America.

LANDSCAPE ARRANGEMENTS. Woodsy, natural-looking designs that juxtapose foliage and flowers, imitating the way they grow in the wild in an attempt to capture a slice of nature. Despite the intent to be natural, landscape arrangements may look "floristy" and contrived if not created by a good florist. Compare with **vegetative arrangements.**

LEAD BOWS. Bows, knots or swags made from strips of soft, malleable dark-gray lead with a flat patina finish; used to accent all kinds of containers, particularly glass vases, terra-cotta pots or trays and baskets.

SHEILA MACQUEEN. A tireless and enthusiastic Englishwoman who travels all over the world teaching people how to arrange flowers in the natural, traditional English way. She uses greenhouse-grown flowers as well as those from the garden or roadsides. Her knowledge of horticulture extends to the garden, and she's keen on encouraging people to grow their own foliage and flowers, with a

268

view to how they can be used in arrangements. She has served as chief decorator and demonstrator for the **Constance Spry** organization, which she joined in 1931; has won many awards, including the Royal Horticultural Society's Victoria Medal of Honor; is the author of a number of books on arranging and gardening; has appeared on several television spots for the BBC; has made a video for home use; and has contributed to various periodicals.

MILLEFLEUR. Literally, "a thousand flowers." A millefleur arrangement is usually taller than it is wide, and is a free composition of numerous varieties of flowers. It's loose and airy but highly textured and vibrant.

MINIMALIST ARRANGEMENTS. Designs that use as little floral material as possible to create a striking, and usually geometric, sculptured effect. Flashy flowers, such as heliconia, proteas, or rubrum lilies, take center stage against a sparse leaf or reed structure. With its inherent airiness, this is the extreme of **high-style arrangements**. The principle here is less is more.

MOOD MOSS. Also called hump moss. A clean, dried sheet of emerald green moss that is shaped around the base of a plant or arrangement, adding an aesthetically pleasing finishing touch to the presentation of the plant.

MOSSED OASIS. A block of green plastic foam covered with moss or combination of mosses. There's an art to knowing how to "moss up"; it takes a deft hand. See also **oasis**.

NEW WAVE ARRANGEMENTS. Abstract designs in which emphasis is on the shape, rather than the natural beauty, of the flower and/or foliage, which is often painted. These floral sculptures often incorporate all kinds of props made from inorganic materials—wire mesh, copper tubing, and plastic glitter stick, for example—look as though they were the subject of a Peter Max design or an Andy Warhol painting.

OASIS. A block of green plastic foam that soaks up water. It may be cut to size and sunk in a container or concealed some other way. Because it is spongelike, flowers can easily be inserted into it for arrangements. Oasis makes the arranging and transporting of flowers a lot easier, because it holds them securely in place. But flowers don't like the material and last a lot longer in plain water. Oasis should be avoided if the life expectancy of cut flowers is an important consideration. See also **mossed oasis.**

PARALLEL ARRANGEMENTS. Designs characterized by multiple growth points. This style is in contrast to traditional designs, in which flowers radiate from one central point. Parallel growth points may be individual, like reeds in a swamp, or they may be clustered, like soldiers in a split formation. Parallelism can get very technical, and even tiresome. For example, if three similar flowers—say, snapdragons—are clustered and there's a bend at the tips of the flowers, then all three blossoms must bend the same way. Whew!

PERENNIALS. Plants that survive the winter months in a dormant state. After the leaves and, usually, the stems die, the roots and any other parts below ground remain very much alive. Perennials are everlasting and flower year after year, at a certain time. Some hardy perennials keep their leaves through the winter. Leaves and stems are soft and fleshy (herbaceous), not woody, distinguishing them from those of trees and bushes. The flowers and foliage, or both, are valuable in landscaping and arranging. Common perennials include iris, peonies, larkspur, columbine, bleeding heart, and asters. A number of mail-order houses are devoted to developing, growing and selling perennials.

PLATEAUXING. Similar to **stacking,** but with more space between the overlapping elements. In the wrong hands, it can look contrived.

PROPRIETARY PRODUCTS. Decorative accessories and floral products that have been designed by a particular shop and made specially for that shop, which usually is the only establishment to sell them. From time to time, however, proprietaries may be carried by other stores.

RAFFIA. A light-tan palm fiber, used to tie flowers for support or simply as a decorative means of securing knots or bows to containers or protective paper around bouquets. It's soft enough not to bruise or cut flower stems.

ROUNDY MOUNDY. A term coined by florists to describe the artless arrangements typical of many wire services. Traditional flowers such as chrysanthemums, carnations and baby's breath are packed into a container, often using oasis, the overall look of which is a symmetrical "round mound" shape. Another florists' term, *flatback special,* is used to describe a similar artless style where the flowers are stretched out horizontally, creating a flat look to the arrangement.

CONSTANCE SPRY (1886–1960). Perhaps the first professional floral designer to stress the importance of one's natural instincts and personal taste. Though she respected the formal rules of flower arranging, she proclaimed: "Never forget that in arranging flowers you have an opportunity to express your own sense of what is beautiful and you should feel free and uninhibited in doing so." An Englishwoman, she started The Constance Spry Flower School in London; had her own shop, Flower Decorations; and designed the flowers for many royal events, including the coronation of Queen Elizabeth II. She was influenced by seventeenth- and eighteenth-century Dutch and Flemish paintings and by Gertrude Jekyll (1843–1932), an English landscape architect.

STACKING. Laying one thing on top of another, such as mushrooms and even certain flowers and leaves, like daisies or cyclamen, to create a layered effect. If the arranger is not careful, this can look very artificial.

TOPIARY. The art of training plants—herb, foliage or flowering— into specific shapes ranging from animals to architectural forms. The term *standard topiary* is applied to a plant trained on a single stem developing into a single round ball, like a stick with a balloon on top. Sometimes the plant is arduously coaxed from a seedling to take the desired shape on its own without support, but more often it is trained on a wire frame mimicking the desired shape.

Not all topiaries are of growing, living plants; cut or dried flowers may be inserted into the desired foam shape, producing a decorative topiary.

VEGETATIVE ARRANGEMENTS. Designs that imitate the more orderly growth of a garden. Classic vegetative arrangements will cluster flowers of the same type and length—a clump of tulips next to a clump of iris, with a cluster of daffodils set in front. The taller flowers are usually in the back and the shorter ones in front, as in a traditional flower bed. This style makes use of **parallel arrangements** and such floral techniques as **clustering** and **stacking**. Also known as *vegetive*. Compare with **landscape arrangements**.

WRAP BOUQUETS. Arranged bouquets of flowers and/or foliage that are wrapped in cellophane or other decorative paper and tied with ribbons or raffia. It does not come with a container; instead, the recipient merely drops the arranged bouquet in his or her own container. This type of gift is less expensive than one already in a container. Upon receiving a wrap bouquet, it is imperative that you cut the stems back half an inch or so before placing them in water.

INDEX